Chuckra Educational

Verbal Reasoning
Types 1 – 21

There are 20 questions of each type (Type 1 to Type 21), with the exception of Type 3 which has 21 questions.

You can work through each type with your child as a familiarisation exercise without timing them

OR

If used as a timed exercise, your child should aim to complete each type (20 questions) in less than 10 minutes for the simpler types and less than 20 minutes for some of the types they find more challenging. On average, they will have about 35 seconds per question in the real exam, which works out to about 12 minutes for 20 questions.

The Verbal Reasoning practice questions in this book can be completed as either standard version (writing the answers in the space provided on the question pages) or multiple-choice (marking the answers on the multiple-choice answer sheets which can be detached from the centre of the book). Multiple-choice is the more commonly used format.

Type 2 continued ...

A B C D E F G H I J K L M N O P Q R S T U V W X Y Z

34. If the code for BITS is XEPO
What is the meaning of DWHB ? [_____]

35. If the code for HOUSE is SLFHV
What is the meaning of XOLDM ? [_____]

36. If the code for EXIST is ICOZB
What is the meaning of TFXAA ? [_____]

37. If the code for CRISP is XIRHK
What is the code for PALM ? [_____]

38. If the code for PROVES is LNKRAO
What is the meaning of XQYGAP ? [_____]

39. If the code for POLL is UTQQ
What is the meaning of QJSI ? [_____]

40. If the code for CAT is XZG
What is the meaning of WLG ? [_____]

Type 3

You have been given four words and three codes. The codes are not necessarily written in the same order as the words and one code is missing. Once you have figured out which word belongs to each code, answer the questions that follow.

PEEL FIST STAG GASP
8739 4587 1226

41. What is the code for LAPSE [_____]

42. What is the code for LEASE [_____]

43. What is the word for the code 87362 [_____]

DEAL PACE LAGS TAGS
3578 1253 9578

44. What is the code for SEALS [_____]

45. What is the code for SATED [_____]

46. What is the word for the code 89572 [_____]

SOAP PAGE GASP TYPE
2891 9781 3514

47. What is the code for SAGE [_____]

48. What is the code for SOPPY [_____]

49. What is the word for the code 1899824 [_____]

CUPS PANG SUCK CAKE
5127 2379 4368

50. What is the code for PACKS [_____]

51. What is the code for GNU [_____]

52. What is the word for the code 2349 [_____]

LAZY GALE YEAR OVER
5216 8967 4627

53. What is the word for the code 462714 [_____]

LAZY GALE YEAR OVER
5216 8967 4627

54. What is the word for the code 9674 [_____]

55. What is the code for LARGE [_____]

GOAT AGES STAG MEAN
4251 2346 7548

56. What is the word for the code 425861 [_____]

57. What is the word for the code 6324 [_____]

58. What is the code for NAMES [_____]

LAMB BOLT MALE BRED
3145 5879 4137

59. What is the word for the code 474578 [_____]

60. What is the word for the code 3189 [_____]

61. What is the code for AMBLE [_____]

In each of the following questions, find the letters that best complete the sentence. The alphabet has been provided to assist you.

A B C D E F G H I J K L M N O P Q R S T U V W X Y Z

EXAMPLE

HU is to FW as ME is to [_____]

Answer : KG

---

62. HD is to BX as KJ is to [_____]

63. WS is to SO as ZG is to [_____]

64. LH is to NJ as QW is to [_____]

65. BX is to AW as ZM is to [_____]

66. IM is to FJ as QK is to [_____]

67. XT is to SO as AZ is to [_____]

68. MJ is to NK as RX is to [_____]

69. BD is to YW as GA is to [_____]

70. CA is to ZX as EF is to [_____]

71. PD is to RF as JB is to [_____]

72. MS is to RX as XQ is to [_____]

73. TH is to WK as PG is to [_____]

74. DC is to CB as RF is to [_____]

75. AQ is to CS as FU is to [_____]

76. OX is to KT as CJ is to [_____]

77. DL is to BJ as RY is to [_____]

78. SB is to WF as JW is to [_____]

79. YV is to BE as WX is to [_____]

80. LP is to KO as BT is to [_____]

81. LL is to KK as EY is to [_____]

In each of the following questions, the word in brackets in the second group must be made from the words outside the brackets in the same way as the word in brackets in the first group is made from the words outside the brackets in the first group. Find the missing word.

EXAMPLE

CLEAN [SAFE] FRESH
ALTAR [_____] CUFFS

Answer : FACT

82. NOVEL [MOVED] NAMED
 VIDEO [_____] BASED

83. TRAIN [INNER] RANGE
 CHAOS [_____] SHAME

84. SPITE [EMPTY] MAYBE
 RAPID [_____] RANGE

85. READS [HEARD] GRAPH
 TRIED [_____] THROW

86. SUGAR [DRAWS] WORDS
 MEDIA [_____] LASTS

87. WIDER [CODED] COULD
 PARTS [_____] CALLS

88. KNOWS [NAMES] SHAME
 SEVEN [_____] SOLVE

89. ABOUT [FAULT] FIELD
 WHEEL [_____] SHELF

90. SIGHT [HINTS] CHAIN
 SHORT [_____] CHAIN

91. LEADS [PLANS] OPENS
 INNER [_____] ALTER

92. EMPTY [STORY] WORKS
 AGAIN [_____] AREAS

93. SIDES [READY] EARLY
 APPLE [_____] BASIS

94. BLAME [TABLE] TRIAL
 EMPTY [_____] EVENT

95. VALUE [VAGUE] GLASS
 WASTE [_____] SUGAR

96. CHEAP [CHIPS] SPLIT
 SADLY [_____] DAILY

97. FRONT [TENDS] IDEAS
 SHARE [_____] CLASS

98. GRAPH [RIGHT] THING
 MOUTH [_____] START

99. SHELF [PHASE] PHASE
 SHOWN [_____] PLOTS

100. CHOSE [CHIPS] PRIME
 LEAST [_____] PLAIN

101. CARRY [TODAY] ADOPT
 BLOCK [_____] DATES

Type 6

In the following questions there are three pairs of words. You must complete the third pair in the same way as the first two pairs.

EXAMPLE

(MINUTE, MENU) (CENTRE, CENT)

(SPIRIT, _____)

Answer : STIR

102. (STARTS, TSAR) (REASON, ERAS)

(ASLEEP, _____)

103. (TRAVEL, TEAR) (REPAIR, RIPE)

(STATED, _____)

104. (MERITS, TERM) (PROMPT, PROP)

(DOUBLE, _____)

105. (DAMAGE, DAME) (RESULT, REST)

(PACKET, _____)

106. (STUPID, STUD) (SECRET, SECT)

(PROVED, _____)

107. (DEBATE, DEBT) (WORKED, WORE)

(CORNER, _____)

108. (TAKING, TANK) (MISUSE, MISS)

(REPEAT, _____)

109. (SOLELY, LOSE) (NAMELY, LANE)

(LESSER, _____)

110. (STATES, TEAT) (SPREAD, PARE)

(PLANET, _____)

111. (POUNDS, SPUN) (ENTITY, YETI)

(WEIGHT, _____)

112. (FORMAT, ROAM) (LITTLE, TILT)

(LABELS, _____)

113. (BOTTLE, BOLT) (BETTER, BEET)

(POWERS, _____)

114. (FASTER, EAST) (PURELY, LURE)

(CRISIS, _____)

Type 6 continued ...

115. (SUITED, DUST) (MODELS, SOME)

(LINEAR, _____)

116. (MODERN, DOME) (SOLELY, LOSE)

(SUBTLE, _____)

117. (GARDEN, DARN) (SUBTLE, TUBE)

(WISHES, _____)

118. (MODERN, DONE) (MATTER, TART)

(HONEST, _____)

119. (CRASH, BASH) (SLAVE, RAVE)

(DRAPE, _____)

120. (CROWD, ROWDY) (BREAD, READY)

(PEARL, _____)

121. (BATE, DATE) (LONE, NONE)

(PINK, _____)

In each of the following questions, you are given a sentence. One of the words is missing three consecutive letters, which on their own make a real word. You need to find the missing letters which will complete the word in capitals in the best way to ensure the sentence makes sense.

EXAMPLE

She said EWELL before she boarded the plane.

Answer : FAR

122. She NED the terrorist before she opened fire.

123. We walked along the SHS looking for shells.

124. Everybody SD and applauded.

125. The fat girl K the last piece of cake.

126. I APACHED the corner slowly.

127. He was not in the ST annoyed.

128. The sound REY reminds me of home.

129. Our only chance is to keep FECTLY still.

130. I looked up at my FRI opposite me in class.

131. Stop MING and sing the words.

132. He TED it over to reveal a scorpion.

133. The match REED after a period of rain.

134. HING will stop me passing the eleven plus!

135. You SH see it when you are ready.

136. It is not WRIT in French.

137. The flat BE was unoccupied.

138. I LAED because my dad tried to dance

139. Her face went as WE as chalk

140. He NR saw them.

141. The day had become MI and overcast.

In each of the following questions, you are given a sentence in which a four letter word is hidden at the end of one word and the beginning of the next word. Find the pair of words that contain a real four letter word.

EXAMPLE

Roger paid over the asking price.

Answer : paid over (dove)

142. The juicy chicken is just ours.

143. See that every muscle is relaxed.

144. Holding to your ideals develops will-power.

145. This is being done even today.

146. Assuming they were very decently kept.

147. Our young lady is Miss Mantel.

148. They all went into the house.

149. Lorry fell asleep at his post.

150. And that chicken is his own.

151. Let them all lean upon him.

152. Listen to what is to follow.

153. My memory is circumstantial and unshaken.

154. You will love staying in here.

155. Dickens also used the article incorrectly.

156. This style is exemplified by Berkeley.

157. The weasels were always the victors.

158. Then I burst out laughing too.

159. Neither of us said a word.

160. Rebecca started painfully with a half-exclamation.

161. Henry looked at her sweet smile.

Type 9

In each of the following questions, you are given two words. Choose one letter that can be moved from the word on the left to the word on the right, making two new words. You cannot rearrange any letters, but the letter that you move can fit anywhere in the second word.

EXAMPLE

BLOCK RAIN

Answer : B (LOCK BRAIN)

162. WRING SEER _____ _____

163. IRATE FLED _____ _____

164. OUNCE COLD _____ _____

165. HONEY FIZZ _____ _____

166. TWINS WEAK _____ _____

167. SWINE TICK _____ _____

168. LATER DIED _____ _____

169. CURVE ENDS _____ _____

170. GROVE THIN _____ _____

171. JAUNT AILS _____ _____

172. WHEAT SORE _____ _____

173. SCOLD FAST _____ _____

174. FLUSH ORE _____ _____

175. VOICE TANG _____ _____

176. LINED RIG _____ _____

177. FOURS AIRS _____ _____

178. LIVER CAVE _____ _____

179. FAMED AIRY _____ _____

180. TWANG HOSE _____ _____

181. SPANK OUCH _____ _____

Type 10

In each of the following questions, find the one letter that will complete the word in front of the brackets and begin the word after the brackets. The same letter must fit into both sets of brackets.

EXAMPLE

STOR (__) AMS   CARR (__) ARD

Answer : Y

182. PEE (__) EVER   OW (__) AX

183. WOL (__) ATS   TUR (__) LAGS

184. LI (__) OMP   CHEA (__) ICKS

185. HAR (__) AMP   ACI (__) ONE

186. FA (__) EEFS   STA (__) OAMS

187. BRE (__) HAT   WO (__) ORK

188. SAL (__) ND   CUR (__) LUDE

189. JO (__) IFT   GA (__) IRL

190. CA (__) IE   CHI (__) HASE

191. WHO (__) USH   FIL (__) ILK

192. CHU (__) OUNT   DEE (__) INT

193. RA (__) OPE   EL (__) ISTS

194. PU (__) HAWS   FLIN (__) RAP

195. CLO (__) ATE   TWI (__) ULLY

196. DENI (__) ISS   SEE (__) ADAM

197. OA (__) LOP   SCAR (__) AN

198. SCAR (__) ILER   GUL (__) LIER

199. FROT (__) ARP   O (__) ATE

200. MEN (__) NSET   YO (__) LCER

201. HO (__) ALM   CRI (__) ASED

Type 11

In each of the following questions, find the two words, one from each group, that together make a new, real word. The word from the group on the left always comes first.

EXAMPLE

(fresh habit mixed)   (acted glass at)

Answer : habitat

202. (they your two)   (self shelf shoe)

203. (world earth sea)   (lie low wide)

204. (job errand work)   (can easy able)

205. (was is will)   (him her his)

206. (guest look visit)   (or and but)

207. (him us you)   (old ten age)

208. (foot walk step)   (sun son soon)

209. (store keep shop)   (space room door)

210. (true valid real)   (ate eat lunch)

211. (middle bottom upper)   (most mist must)

212. (over under next)   (square dot line)

213. (truth lies honest)   (fully ally empty)

214. (card trick joke)   (follow led front)

215. (run sit stand)   (by bye buy)

216. (row road track)   (tie suit belt)

217. (to too at)   (night moon star)

218. (between through thought)   (under in out)

219. (the some one)   (me you him)

220. (as that then)   (queen king jack)

221. (tea hot drink)   (rung wrong ring)

Type 12

For each of the following questions, find two words, one from each group that are most opposite in meaning.

EXAMPLE

(low pump sell) (king high bottom)

Answer : low high

222. (font back above) (front slide black)

223. (upstairs house ceiling) (outside floor building)

224. (coward fight custard) (food safe hero)

225. (living animal keeper) (extinct forest wild)

226. (theatre cry comedy) (joke laugh tear)

227. (sweet taste cute) (nose tongue sour)

228. (sea sink bath) (float plug water)

229. (talk court truth) (stand lie detector)

230. (ease attempt difficult) (test divide easy)

231. (push open door) (close handle near)

232. (awake night bed) (snore asleep sheet)

233. (uniform dress naked) (clothed cloth cool)

234. (tops stop spot) (start shop star)

235. (speed run slow) (plane fast wing)

236. (compass north mouth) (direction magnetic south)

237. (temperature hot water) (sun cold weather)

238. (bold bald balk) (heavy hairy hardy)

239. (best beat bear) (worst worth wart)

240. (batter better bitter) (sweep swede sweet)

241. (scrub clear clean) (dirty dry deny)

Type 13

For each of the following questions, find two words, one from each group, that are most similar in meaning.

EXAMPLE

(save jump sell) (king keep hero)

Answer : save keep

242. (bucket beaker bouquet) (cup breaker beak)

243. (medicine ache pill) (head spot pain)

244. (borough town bough) (meadow branch bird)

245. (dinner broken broth) (soup cook brother)

246. (bunk leave night) (leaf hammock sheet)

247. (meal meat cafeteria) (restaurant drink eat)

248. (rival canal friend) (canary river ship)

249. (chair stood floor) (cheer stool man)

250. (champ chimp chum) (fiend friend chump)

251. (note forger counter) (counterfeiter feet money)

252. (brush hairdresser comb) (tools barbaric barber)

253. (comedy club giggle) (good goggles laugh)

254. (obese fit object) (boiler fat gym)

255. (trip snare drum) (trap ear part)

256. (abandon band anon) (leave holiday tree)

257. (abbey abyss abbot) (charm charcoal chasm)

258. (reverse gear advance) (move progress prong)

259. (afraid knot frayed) (frightened city bent)

260. (meant amend amenity) (chance change charge)

261. (amiable flight find) (friendly fiend fierce)

Type 14

For each of the following questions, find the two words that are different from the other three.

EXAMPLE

octopus lion shark elephant eel

Answer : lion elephant

262. aluminium wood steel tin plastic

263. sailor archbishop postman vicar priest

264. gorilla chimpanzee cage monkey zoo

265. address car street avenue road

266. piano violin music trumpet note

267. queen pauper emperor king reign

268. up front side back keeper

269. rhubarb hydrogen liquid oxygen helium

270. mother family daughter uncle relate

271. daughter sun rock planet moon

272. lake side pond thames river

273. neck goose water swan duck

274. ash forest oak elm fire

275. gaze eyes run look stare

276. rugby field cricket player tennis

277. cut hammer chisel saw wood

278. carrots sprouts peas cream soup

279. ace game king queen paper

280. baked roasted food boiled oven

281. weather breeze gale plane hurricane

Type 15

In each of the following questions you must choose two words, one from each group in brackets, that best complete the sentence.

EXAMPLE

Pip is to (squeak, orange, red)
as stone is to (plumb, pebble, plum).

Answer : orange plum

282.   Foot is to (fool, sock, inch)
as hand is to (finger, stock, glove).

283.   Kitten is to (cat, play, tail)
as lamb is to (large, sheep, dip).

284.   Square is to (cool, four, fore)
as triangle is to (three, instrument, music).

285.   Emerald is to (green, fair, isle)
as ruby is to (curry, red, wax).

286.   Leopard is to (lion, line, spots)
as zebra is to (stripes, crossing, plain).

287.   Train is to (exercise, rail, book)
as bus is to (pass, road, stop).

288.   Leg is to (foot, lent, left)
as arm is to (less, hand, more).

289.   Cat is to (feed, feline, catch)
as dog is to (car, biscuit, canine).

290.   Cent is to (central, hall, dollar)
as pence is to (spent, pound, money).

291.   Scale is to (fish, weight, music)
as feather is to (bird, flight, nest).

292.   Nephew is to (relative, uncle, unclean)
as niece is to (nice, taunt, aunt).

293.   Squeak is to (mouse, trap, house)
as roar is to (oar, lion, noise).

294.   Prisoner is to (free, jail, rock)
as patient is to (hospital, careful, medicine).

295.   Floor is to (ceiling, wooden, horizontal)
as wall is to (flower, street, vertical).

Type 15 continued ...

296.   Pen is to (ink, well, penny)
as pencil is to (draw, lead, sharpen).

297.   Pork is to (poor, pig, fork)
as venison is to (deer, cook, venus).

298.   Viewer is to (television, aerial, colour)
as listener is to (hear, radio, ear).

299.   Breakfast is to (egg, morning, flake)
as supper is to (super, evening, slipper).

300.   Pots is to (go, stop, move)
as star is to (rats, mice, film).

301.   Solar is to (sun, star, mirror)
as lunar is to (planet, satellite, moon).

In the questions below, there are two pairs of words. Choose the word from the five possible answers which goes equally well with both the pairs.

EXAMPLE

(relax, sleep) (remainder, others)

Answer : rest

302.   (group, gang) (gather, congregate)

class crowd hunt gaggle collect

303.   (flames, blaze) (dismiss, sack)

hot fire ignore hire burn

304.   (slender, slim) (prop, rest)

thin support lean faint tired

305.   (escalated, grew) (dandelion, pansy)

rose ascended daisy soar leaf

306.   (glow, shine) (faint, delicate)

cute blush frail gleam light

307.   (cow, bull) (thigh, shin)

sigh foot cattle calf animal

308.   (eagle, pigeon) (gulp, ingest)

finch swallow sip absorb glide

309.   (crouch, dodge) (drake, bird)

duck avoid gander miss swim

310.   (soar, hover) (bee, wasp)

hornet fly swoop flee circle

311.   (earl, baron) (calculate, compute)

count confess tally countess viscount

312.   (trinket, mascot) (attract, allure)

fascinate charm bracelet magic artichoke

313.   (rind, shell) (strip, exfoliate)

streak hind shave husk peel

314.   (end, point) (pour, spill)

tip peak lean money pill

315.   (boost, elevate) (journey, ride)

descend shaft lift car floor

316.   (bun, bread) (rotate, wheel)

butter roll revolve turn scone

317.   (confuse, bewilder) (hurl, fling)

baffle heave throw swat lob

318.   (crust, coat) (yap, howl)

bark roar case snarl bellow

319.   (complimentary, costless) (idle, vacant)

clear free unpaid open busy

320.   (gale, breeze) (coil, meander)

bind wind bond wand bend

321.   (component, portion) (split, separate)

screw part pin party divorce

Type 17

For each of the following questions, numbers have been allocated to letters. Work out the answer to the sum and mark the appropriate letter on the answer sheet or in the space provided.

EXAMPLE

A = 3, B = 6, C = 23, D = 9, E = 31

B x D - C = [___]

Answer : E

322. A = 7, B = 2, C = 9, D = 6, E = 4

D - E + B = [____]

323. A = 5, B = 7, C = 3, D = 2, E = 6

C x D - E + A = [____]

324. A = 6, B = 5, C = 2, D = 1, E = 3

A ÷ E x C - D = [____]

325. A = 9, B = 8, C = 4, D = 2, E = 1

B ÷ C + E - D = [____]

326. A = 3, B = 8, C = 1, D = 6, E = 4

B ÷ E + C = [____]

327. A = 1, B = 4, C = 5, D = 2, E = 6

C - E + D = [____]

328. A = 1, B = 2, C = 8, D = 4, E = 3

C x A ÷ B + D = [____]

329. A = 5, B = 4, C = 1, D = 3, E = 2

A - D + E = [____]

330. A = 6, B = 5, C = 2, D = 9, E = 1

D + C - A = [____]

331. A = 7, B = 9, C = 8, D = 4, E = 2

C x E - B = [____]

332. A = 9, B = 2, C = 1, D = 4, E = 3

B x D + C = [____]

333. A = 1, B = 6, C = 2, D = 5, E = 8

C ÷ A - D + E = [____]

334. A = 1, B = 7, C = 8, D = 6, E = 2

A x E + D = [____]

335. A = 6, B = 8, C = 4, D = 3, E = 5

D + A - E = [____]

Type 17 continued ...

336. A = 4, B = 2, C = 7, D = 8, E = 3

B x A + E - D = [____]

337. A = 39, B = 44, C = 45, D = 33, E = 21

C + D - A = [____]

338. A = 30, B = 15, C = 9, D = 2, E = 10

B x D - A + E = [____]

339. A = 42, B = 49, C = 19, D = 10, E = 40

C - D + E = [____]

340. A = 33, B = 40, C = 47, D = 9, E = 31

C + A - B = [____]

341. A = 9, B = 29, C = 31, D = 26, E = 34

E + D - B = [____]

Type 18

For each of the following questions, find the number that best completes the series.

EXAMPLE

Example 12 12 13 15 18 [___]

Answer : 22

342. 15, 9, 15, 11, 16, 13, 18, [___]

343. 20, 19, 18, 17, 16, 15, 14, [___]

344. 2, 2, 4, 12, 48, [___]

345. 6, 7, 9, 12, 16, 21, 27, [___]

346. 6, 12, 24, 48, 96, [___]

347. 5, 8, 11, 14, 17, 20, 23, [___]

348. 10, 11, 13, 16, 20, 25, 31, [___]

349. 3, 16, 4, 17, 5, 19, 6, 22, 7, [___]

350. 15, 13, 11, 9, 7, 5, 3, [___]

351. 9, 3, 10, 5, 12, 7, 15, 9, 19, [___]

352. 21, 10, 22, 10, 24, 10, 27, 10, 31, [___]

353. 1024, 512, 256, 128, 64, [___]

354. 15, 18, 22, 27, 33, 40, 48, [___]

355. 39, 3, 40, 6, 41, 10, 42, 15, 43, [___]

356. 4, 2, 7, 4, 11, 7, 16, 11, 22, [___]

357. 35, 7, 35, 8, 36, 9, 38, 10, 41, [___]

358. 27, 30, 34, 39, 45, 52, 60, [___]

359. 21, 1, 24, 1, 27, 2, 30, 4, 33, [___]

360. 18, 15, 19, 13, 21, 11, 24, 9, 28, [___]

361. 12, 13, 15, 18, 22, 27, 33, [___]

Type 19

In each of the following questions, the numbers in the third group must be related to each other in the same way as the numbers in each of the other two groups. Find the missing number.

EXAMPLE

(3 [12] 4) (7 [35] 5) (9 [____] 2)

Answer : 18

362. (12 [32] 20) (14 [38] 24) (10 [___] 4)

363. (48 [89] 34) (16 [29] 6) (24 [___] 9)

364. (30 [32] 1) (33 [43] 5) (37 [___] 32)

365. (43 [52] 18) (30 [70] 49) (13 [___] 38)

366. (41 [78] 37) (28 [54] 26) (36 [___] 38)

367. (47 [105] 11) (37 [102] 28) (5 [___] 29)

368. (36 [96] 30) (48 [64] 8) (34 [___] 13)

369. (38 [90] 26) (39 [89] 25) (40 [___] 26)

370. (20 [51] 29) (13 [17] 2) (25 [___] 40)

371. (6 [8] 2) (22 [26] 4) (23 [___] 21)

372. (22 [30] 8) (4 [31] 27) (12 [___] 23)

373. (6 [25] 14) (24 [37] 8) (23 [___] 10)

374. (5 [33] 28) (22 [34] 12) (11 [___] 12)

375. (6 [42] 15) (3 [44] 19) (10 [___] 29)

376. (17 [25] 17) (13 [10] 6) (20 [___] 11)

377. (11 [30] 15) (19 [50] 27) (20 [___] 12)

378. (10 [56] 18) (3 [14] 4) (18 [___] 2)

379. (11 [25] 3) (10 [44] 24) (1 [___] 10)

380. (3 [12] 3) (21 [68] 13) (25 [___] 15)

381. (12 [70] 23) (14 [80] 26) (7 [___] 28)

CHUCKRA EDUCATIONAL

Verbal Reasoning Practice Book1 - Parent's notes and Answer Booklet

PLEASE DETACH THESE PAGES FROM THE CENTRE OF THE BOOK

- The Multiple Choice Answer Sheets
- A Guide for Parents
- The Correct Answers

Note: In the real exam, the multiple choice answer sheet is separate from the question paper.

Use the table on the following page to record your child's progress through the book.

To calculate the test result as a percentage:

100 × Number of Q's Correct ÷ Total Number of Q's in Test

GENERAL ADVICE WHEN TAKING A TEST:

- Write down the exact time you start so you can work out how much time has elapsed at any point during the test.

- Make sure that you can see a clock or have your own watch to keep an eye on your timing.

- Read the instructions for each section carefully.

- Using the multiple-choice answer sheets:

  o Mark your answers in pencil with a clear horizontal line across the whole width of the appropriate box or boxes.

  o Ensure you have a good eraser to rub out any answers you wish to change. You may NOT cross out an answer!

  o You must NOT do any working out or write notes on the multiple-choice answer sheet. All working should be done on the <u>question paper</u> or a piece of spare paper.

- Each question is worth only one mark. Therefore, if you are struggling to answer a question, take a guess and then put a star next the question on your <u>question paper</u> so you can remember to come back to it at the end, if you have time.

Good luck!

PROGRESS RECORD

TEST	Number of Q's CORRECT	TOTAL Number of Questions	Result in %	TIME TAKEN
TYPE 1		20		
TYPE 2		20		
TYPE 3		21		
TYPE 4		20		
TYPE 5		20		
TYPE 6		20		
TYPE 7		20		
TYPE 8		20		
TYPE 9		20		
TYPE 10		20		
TYPE 11		20		
TYPE 12		20		
TYPE 13		20		
TYPE 14		20		
TYPE 15		20		
TYPE 16		20		
TYPE 17		20		
TYPE 18		20		
TYPE 19		20		
TYPE 20		20		
TYPE 21		20		
ASSESSMENT TEST 1		80		
ASSESSMENT TEST 2		80		

Multiple Choice Answer Sheet for Verbal Reasoning Types 1 - 21

T1 Ex.
- OV
- OC —
- CO
- VC
- CB

Q1
- BP
- BT
- VR
- GS
- GV

Q2
- IV
- VP
- OP
- PT
- PV

Q3
- PP
- JN
- WR
- CT
- BZ

Q4
- JN
- DT
- WR
- CZ
- QP

Q5
- YT
- NL
- ML
- NP
- KN

Q6
- XS
- BE
- EU
- RQ
- YS

Q7
- VS
- VW
- WS
- LO
- VQ

Q8
- YS
- SQ
- HV
- IX
- PZ

Q9
- ZP
- TK
- PZ
- KR
- RK

Q10
- IE
- WT
- IX
- DV
- QR

Q11
- QR
- JJ
- JK
- KX
- XT

Q12
- KX
- RR
- XT
- RN
- EW

Q13
- RS
- LQ
- EW
- YU
- IO

Q14
- SS
- ZU
- UQ
- FL
- UL

Q15
- MQ
- GO
- IU
- TS
- IH

Q16
- UB
- AV
- NQ
- TS
- GO

Q17
- AV
- GP
- NR
- BK
- UT

Q18
- AN
- HP
- OR
- MG
- UT

Q19
- IS
- IP
- BN
- ST
- OS

Q20
- CN
- OB
- VL
- OR
- IP

T2 Ex.
- LOUT
- LOOP —
- LOSE
- TREE
- LAME

Q21
- TQKH
- TSKH
- MQKH
- TQKN
- TQIH

Q22
- UDAT
- ADTT
- AMAT
- ADAT
- ADATM

Q23
- CFIAXJJ
- CEBAXJJ
- CEIVXJJ
- CEIARJJ
- CEIAXJJ

Q24
- VICE
- DEEP
- WISE
- HARD
- GETS

Q25
- CQBZWMK
- BCBZWMK
- CCBZWMK
- CCOZWMK
- CCBZGMK

Q26
- POWERS
- POUNDS
- JOINED
- FAIRLY
- POLICY

Q27
- JSGFTBF
- ATGFTBF
- ASGFTBF
- ASGOTBF
- ASGFNBF

Q28
- LOADED
- MOTHER
- HORSES
- QUOTES
- SEEING

Q29
- SENDING
- HAPPILY
- HAPPENS
- HARMFUL
- UNCLEAR

Q30
- HMSXGU
- YMSXGU
- YKSXGU
- YMSIGU
- YMIXGU

Q31
- HYJLX
- PLJLX
- PYXLX
- PYJXX
- PYJLX

Q32
- OZULA
- IHLQU
- OFXPB
- PWTYH
- IFXOB

Q33
- ACTUAL
- WHILST
- ACTION
- MEMORY
- ACTIVE

Q34
- HAVE
- MAIL
- TALK
- HALF
- HATE

Q35
- GROWL
- CLOWN
- SMART
- CLOUD
- SMILE

Q36
- PAUSE
- PARTS
- MINDS
- LEVEL
- SCENE

Q37
- KHLS
- KZON
- KPJZ
- TRSA
- TOMV

Q38
- BUCKET
- BUTTON
- FACTOR
- FUTURE
- PASSED

Q39
- SEES
- LESS
- LOGS
- LETS
- LEND

Q40
- DOG
- BUG
- DOT
- POT
- DIG

T3 Ex.
No example for this type

Q41
- 63185
- 86964
- 46441
- 74852
- 63182

Q42
- 17382
- 62382
- 99823
- 66758
- 17392

Q43
- ZINC
- STALE
- HALES
- MALES
- GALES

Q44
- 87597
- 82538
- 63524
- 63792
- 67583

Q45
- 96875
- 85921
- 45623
- 85932
- 85882

Q46
- DISCS
- STAGE
- TAPER
- PAPER
- PARTS

Q47
- 9884
- 9824
- 9825
- 8172
- 1824

Q48
- 11111
- 92115
- 97115
- 96115
- 97195

Q49
- MESSAGE
- BRIDGES
- PASSIVE
- PASSAGE
- PASSERS

Q50
- 43275
- 43271
- 48875
- 43215
- 34271

Q51
- 831
- 862
- 312
- 168
- 861

Q52
- CAME
- MAST
- CAST
- CAPS
- CAPE

Q53
- PEARLY
- NEARLY
- YEARLY
- GROOVY
- YEARNS

Q54
- KIDS
- VARY
- VERY
- SWAM
- STAR

Q55
- 13284
- 12756
- 12759
- 12985
- 12984

Q56
- AGENTS
- SPARES
- ACTIVE
- AGREES
- STINGS

Q57
- BOAT
- TOAD
- DOGS
- GOAT
- TOGA

Q58
- 24751
- 84751
- 84721
- 82751
- 98832

Q59
- MEMBER
- MOTIVE
- MINGLE
- SNATCH
- MEMORY

Q60
- HARD
- LARD
- CARD
- WARD
- DRUM

Q61
- 19537
- 14536
- 64537
- 12537
- 14537

T4 Ex.
- KF
- QW
- YH
- HR
- KG —

Q62
- CQ
- UE
- EU
- ED
- WO

Q63
- CQ
- VS
- VC
- QU
- WO

Q64
- WO
- DQ
- SY
- KT
- QN

Q65
- QN
- XP
- YL
- ER
- KT

Q66
- KT
- NH
- RN
- YP
- ER

Q67
- UV
- VU
- LT
- SN
- UP

Q68
- SY
- YP
- FR
- ML
- SN

Q69
- MM
- TO
- TZ
- ZQ
- SN

Q70
- SV
- UP
- GS
- UV
- GK

Q71
- GK
- NL
- LD
- LO
- LQ

Q72
- HK
- NM
- UO
- CV
- BI

Q73
- BI
- HK
- SJ
- RX
- YR

Q74
- YR
- FT
- LV
- SP
- QE

Q75
- HW
- ZR
- FT
- MV
- TP

Q76
- ZR
- GT
- NV
- TQ
- YF

Q77	Q78	Q79	Q80	Q81	T5 Ex.	Q82	Q83	Q84	Q85
PW	NA	IJ	VQ	DX	FACT —	DICED	OASES	BRINK	BINGE
AS	UQ	DQ	CY	PO	DOGS	SADLE	OTTER	DRINK	GROWL
GU	MZ	BS	GY	WR	MAKE	TIDES	BEAVER	DRAIN	WRITE
NO	HU	IM	IM	CL	FACE	SIDED	HONES	GRAIN	WIRES
UQ	OO	DC	GM	JN	DIGS	RIFFS	CONES	PLANE	PYRES

Q86	Q87	Q88	Q89	Q90	Q91	Q92	Q93
TAILS	MARKS	PLANT	FROGS	MINTS	BLUNT	WIRES	SLAPS
SNAIL	GRIDS	FROWN	SWELL	HINTS	LINKS	PARTS	MAPLE
GRAIL	DARTS	BROWN	FORKS	KILTS	LINEN	STOPS	DRUGS
NAILS	MONKS	ELVES	SPELL	BRAND	LINER	GRAPE	MOUSE
SALES	CARTS	ELVIS	DRIVE	GRAND	GRAVE	SIREN	CHAPS

Q94	Q95	Q96	Q97	Q98	Q99	Q100	Q101
TURTLE	SOUND	LABEL	DROPS	HOUSE	PHOTO	CRAWL	STALK
HELPS	HASTE	SABLE	EARLS	OATHS	BRINK	SPELL	LACKS
TELLS	TASTE	MILKS	PEARL	ROAST	GRIDS	SPIEL	WACKS
GRAVY	ROUND	THROW	GIRLS	ETHER	PLANS	STEAL	WAXED
ENEMY	WASTE	SALAD	SALTY	HEATH	JUICE	LEAPS	CHALK

T6 Ex.	Q102	Q103	Q104	Q105	Q106	Q107	Q108	Q109	Q110
WRAP	SALE	TEAS	LOBE	PACK	PROD	CORN	PEAR	SELL	LANE
STAR	PEEL	EATS	LOUD	PALE	PORE	CONE	REAP	LESS	LATE
STIR —	LEAP	SEAT	BELL	TACT	ROVE	CORE	PEER	REEL	LEAN
STOP	APES	EAST	BLED	PACT	ROAP	COPE	PARE	LEER	PANT
RATS	PALS	SATE	DOLE	CAPE	DOVE	HORN	PRAY	EELS	LAMP

Q111	Q112	Q113	Q114	Q115	Q116	Q117	Q118	Q119
GIRL	BALL	PORE	ISIS	REAL	STUB	HISS	TONE	PEAR
TWIN	BELL	POOR	IRIS	REEL	BUST	DISH	NEST	CARE
LINE	SLAB	PEWS	SIRS	RILE	LUTE	SUSHI	NOTS	CAPE
LIST	BALE	POSE	MISS	RAIN	TUBS	HILL	NOSE	PAIR
TWIG	SALE	POPS	KISS	LIER	BUTS	SHIP	NOTE	AREA

Q120	Q121	T7 Ex.	Q122	Q123	Q124	Q125	Q126	Q127	Q128
REALLY	KINK	AND	SAD	ORE	FIR	SIP	PRO	VAN	WON
EARLY	RINSE	TOP	DID	DOG	TOO	EMU	FED	PUB	RID
LEARN	RANK	TIN	WHY	PET	LAP	ICY	GUN	TON	ASS
PLANE	RINK	FAR —	WAR	RHO	URN	TOO	CUP	LEA	ALL
PLAY	NICE	EWE	BID	WIT	HOP	DIE	SAW	FUN	RUN

Q129	Q130	Q131	Q132	Q133	Q134	Q135	Q136	Q137	Q138	Q139
RUT	YAM	PAY	URN	SUM	RUG	ILL	FAR	GEM	MUM	LID
NUB	VEX	FIG	INK	MEN	CUD	ALL	TEN	LOW	WEB	COB
RUG	DRY	HUM	SKY	YET	ICE	FIT	YAM	PIG	UGH	HIT
PER	END	JUG	MUM	DAB	NOT	FIG	MUD	PLY	HID	INK
USE	ILL	FAG	YAM	ELL	YEW	LOP	NIB	ROD	ANA	JUG

Q140	Q141	T8 Ex.	Q142	Q143	Q144	Q145
GOD	HAY	Roger paid	The juicy	See that	Holding to	This is
EVE	STY	paid over —	juicy chicken	that every	to your	is being
TAG	HEW	over the	chicken is	every muscle	your ideals	being done
WAR	MAP	the asking	is just	muscle is	ideals develops	done even
HAG	YAP	asking price	just ours	is relaxed	develops will-power	even today

Q146
Assuming they
they were
were very
very decently
decently kept

Q147
Our young
young lady
lady is
is Miss
Miss Mantel

Q148
They all
all went
went into
into the
the house

Q149
Lorry fell
fell asleep
asleep at
at his
his post

Q150
And that
that chicken
chicken is
is his
his own

Q151
Let them
them all
all lean
lean upon
upon him

Q152
Listen to
to what
what is
is to
to follow

Q153
My memory
memory is
is circumstantial
circumstantial and
and unshaken

Q154
You will
will love
love staying
staying in
in here

Q155
Dickens also
also used
used the
the article
article incorrectly

Q156
This style
style is
is exemplified
exemplified by
by Berkeley

Q157
The Weasels
Weasels were
were always
always the
the victors

Q158
Then I
I burst
burst out
out laughing
laughing too

Q159
Neither of
of us
us said
said a
a word

Q160
Rebecca started
started painfully
painfully with
with a
a half-exclamation

Q161
Henry looked
looked at
at her
her sweet
sweet smile

T9 Ex.
B —
L
O
C
K

Q162
W
R
I
N
G

Q163
I
R
A
T
E

Q164
O
U
N
C
E

Q165
H
O
N
E
Y

Q166
T
W
I
N
S

Q167
S
W
I
N
E

Q168
L
A
T
E
R

Q169
C
U
R
V
E

Q170
G
R
O
V
E

Q171
J
A
U
N
T

Q172
W
H
E
A
T

Q173
S
C
O
L
D

Q174
F
L
U
S
H

Q175
V
O
I
C
E

Q176
L
I
N
E
D

Q177
F
O
U
R
S

Q178
L
I
V
E
R

Q179
F
A
M
E
D

Q180
T
W
A
N
G

Q181
S
P
A
N
K

T10 Ex.
T
E
Y —
S
J

Q182
T
L
S
M
I

Q183
L
F
K
U
G

Q184
L
N
P
J
U

Q185
Y
P
I
D
H

Q186
G
Q
R
B
J

Q187
U
B
O
W
N

Q188
D
E
T
A
K

Q189
W
Y
G
N
L

Q190
Q
P
M
Y
B

Q191
W
R
S
M
G

Q192
E
J
F
M
D

Q193
M
O
S
C
T

Q194
T
L
V
G
E

Q195
U
Y
O
G
P

Q196
I
A
T
M
G

Q197
M
F
O
D
L

Q198
H
P
F
K
Y

Q199
H
F
I
S
L

Q200
D
B
N
U
E

Q201
Y
B
R
P
G

T11 Ex.
fresh   acted
habit —   glass
mixed   at —

Q202
they   self
your   shelf
two   shoe

Q203
world   lie
earth   low
sea   wide

Q204
job   can
errand   easy
work   able

Q205
was   him
is   her
will   his

Q206
guest   or
look   and
visit   but

Q207
him   old
us   ten
you   age

Q208
foot   sun
walk   son
step   soon

Q209
store   space
keep   room
shop   door

Q210
true   ate
valid   eat
real   lunch

Q211
middle   most
bottom   mist
upper   must

Q212
over   square
under   dot
next   line

Q213
truth   fully
lies   ally
honest   empty

Q214
card   follow
trick   led
joke   front

Q215
run   by
sit   bye
stand   buy

Q216
row   tie
road   suit
track   belt

Q217
to   night
too   moon
at   star

Q218
between under
through in
thought out

Q219
the   me
some   you
one   him

Q220
as   queen
that   king
then   jack

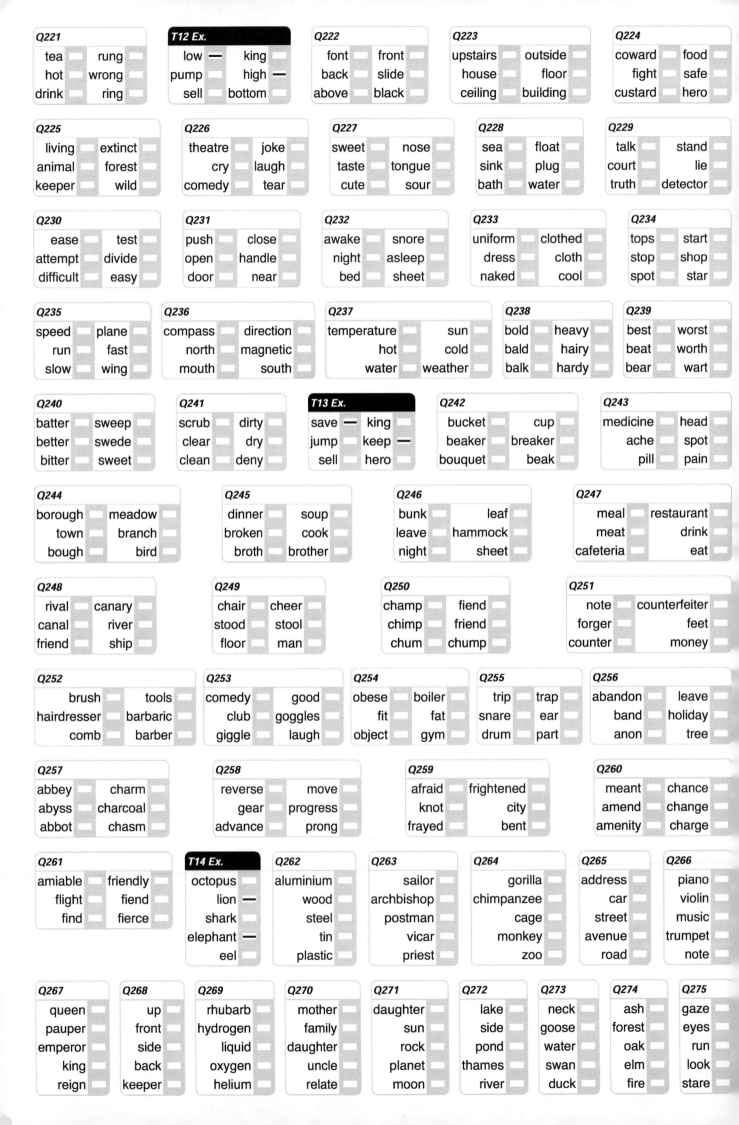

Q221
tea · rung
hot · wrong
drink · ring

T12 Ex.
low — king
pump · high —
sell · bottom

Q222
font · front
back · slide
above · black

Q223
upstairs · outside
house · floor
ceiling · building

Q224
coward · food
fight · safe
custard · hero

Q225
living · extinct
animal · forest
keeper · wild

Q226
theatre · joke
cry · laugh
comedy · tear

Q227
sweet · nose
taste · tongue
cute · sour

Q228
sea · float
sink · plug
bath · water

Q229
talk · stand
court · lie
truth · detector

Q230
ease · test
attempt · divide
difficult · easy

Q231
push · close
open · handle
door · near

Q232
awake · snore
night · asleep
bed · sheet

Q233
uniform · clothed
dress · cloth
naked · cool

Q234
tops · start
stop · shop
spot · star

Q235
speed · plane
run · fast
slow · wing

Q236
compass · direction
north · magnetic
mouth · south

Q237
temperature · sun
hot · cold
water · weather

Q238
bold · heavy
bald · hairy
balk · hardy

Q239
best · worst
beat · worth
bear · wart

Q240
batter · sweep
better · swede
bitter · sweet

Q241
scrub · dirty
clear · dry
clean · deny

T13 Ex.
save — king
jump · keep —
sell · hero

Q242
bucket · cup
beaker · breaker
bouquet · beak

Q243
medicine · head
ache · spot
pill · pain

Q244
borough · meadow
town · branch
bough · bird

Q245
dinner · soup
broken · cook
broth · brother

Q246
bunk · leaf
leave · hammock
night · sheet

Q247
meal · restaurant
meat · drink
cafeteria · eat

Q248
rival · canary
canal · river
friend · ship

Q249
chair · cheer
stood · stool
floor · man

Q250
champ · fiend
chimp · friend
chum · chump

Q251
note · counterfeiter
forger · feet
counter · money

Q252
brush · tools
hairdresser · barbaric
comb · barber

Q253
comedy · good
club · goggles
giggle · laugh

Q254
obese · boiler
fit · fat
object · gym

Q255
trip · trap
snare · ear
drum · part

Q256
abandon · leave
band · holiday
anon · tree

Q257
abbey · charm
abyss · charcoal
abbot · chasm

Q258
reverse · move
gear · progress
advance · prong

Q259
afraid · frightened
knot · city
frayed · bent

Q260
meant · chance
amend · change
amenity · charge

Q261
amiable · friendly
flight · fiend
find · fierce

T14 Ex.
octopus
lion —
shark
elephant —
eel

Q262
aluminium
wood
steel
tin
plastic

Q263
sailor
archbishop
postman
vicar
priest

Q264
gorilla
chimpanzee
cage
monkey
zoo

Q265
address
car
street
avenue
road

Q266
piano
violin
music
trumpet
note

Q267
queen
pauper
emperor
king
reign

Q268
up
front
side
back
keeper

Q269
rhubarb
hydrogen
liquid
oxygen
helium

Q270
mother
family
daughter
uncle
relate

Q271
daughter
sun
rock
planet
moon

Q272
lake
side
pond
thames
river

Q273
neck
goose
water
swan
duck

Q274
ash
forest
oak
elm
fire

Q275
gaze
eyes
run
look
stare

11 PLUS PREPARATION ADVICE

Competition to pass the 11+ exam is increasing each year as more and more students are being tutored. As a private tutor, I have successfully helped many children prepare for the 11+ exam. A large proportion of the preparation can, and should, be done prior to the year leading up to the exam if you have time on your side. Initially, the emphasis should be on developing your child's core skills rather than actual exam preparation. If you are reading this with not much time available prior to the exam, then you will need to focus on the actual question types which are likely to appear in the exam itself.

About the 11 Plus Exam

The 11 Plus Exam differs slightly in each county, however most counties use one or a combination of the following disciplines: Verbal Reasoning, Non-Verbal Reasoning, 11+ Maths, 11+ English. You should therefore ascertain which disciplines are used in your county and whether they will be multiple-choice or standard format.

The exam result your child needs to obtain is not actually a set percentage of the exam paper, but rather a score in the top so many percent of all the children taking the 11 Plus Exam for that region. At the end of the day, there are only a certain number of places at Grammar Schools so the scores are adjusted to ensure that only *that* number of places will be filled.

Your child's actual scores will be standardised (adjusted) according to a number of criteria such as their age and how many students have scored above or below them in the test etc. The exact standardisation process is not publicly available, but in essence the scores will be adjusted to give a final result and this is often not reported as a percentage. However, a good benchmark for your child to work towards is consistently scoring over 90% on practice papers.

In total there are 21 types of Verbal Reasoning questions which tend to come up in the current 11 Plus Verbal Reasoning Exam. Each individual paper usually contains 11 to 13 of those types i.e. it is very unlikely that all of the 21 types will appear in one exam paper.

These 21 question types can be categorised into three main groups; vocabulary dependent questions, arithmetic based questions and code-style questions. Around 50% of the question types are vocabulary dependent, 25% are arithmetic based and 25% are code-style. Therefore it is highly beneficial for your child to increase their vocabulary and improve their arithmetic skills when preparing for the 11 Plus Verbal Reasoning Exam.

It is important to realise that although these 21 question types have been used in the Verbal Reasoning exams for many years, there is the slight possibility that a few of the question types (or even all of them) may change. Although unlikely, you do have to realise this is a possibility. To cover this eventuality, it is important to ensure your child's core skills are strong and not focus solely on these questions types. We have a selection of other materials on our website to help improve your child's core skills as well as additional verbal reasoning practice questions.

The challenge in the 11 Plus Exam is the time factor. Many students can manage to do fairly well when working without a time limit, however the ability to perform under time pressure and still be accurate is where the true challenge lies. One area that catches many students out is not knowing the meaning of a word or recognising whether a word is correctly spelt or even if it is a real word. Use of a dictionary is not permitted during the exam.

The 11+ Verbal Reasoning paper is usually 80 questions to be completed in 50 minutes. This equates to an average of 37.5 seconds per question. You will see, as you complete the questions in this book, some questions can be done in less than 5 seconds each and others take a lot longer.

Chuckra approach to preparation

Avoid the temptation to dive straight into doing full practice papers. We suggest that you start by working through all of the 21 types, ensuring that there is no type your child does not understand. At the same time, make sure to improve your child's core skills (vocabulary, arithmetic, accuracy and speed of mental processing) through a number of other exercises. Try including games as part of the preparation. If preparation is too intense from the beginning, students tend to 'peak' too early and are absolutely exhausted and sick of verbal reasoning by the time of the exam. Pace preparation so your child hits their peak on the day of the exam.

What can you do to support your child?

- Vocabulary

  There is no clearly defined list of vocabulary that is likely to appear in the verbal reasoning papers so one can never sit back and assume your child knows enough words. I am not saying this to cause panic, but to ensure you realise that constantly building your child's vocabulary is hugely beneficial. This is something that should be started as early as possible as a large vocabulary cannot be learnt in a week.

  You should have a system in place to ensure that your child is learning at least 3-5 new words daily and being quizzed on these regularly. In addition to encouraging your child to read a wide range of literature, a good place to start is playing the Chuckra Card games in the alphaCards and voCards and ensuring that any unknown words are added to a wordlist to review later. Please visit our website for useful vocabulary building games and other resources.

- Arithmetic

  The Maths questions that tend to appear in Verbal Reasoning papers focus on the core arithmetic skills such as addition, subtraction, multiplication, division, sequences (number patterns) and word problems, some of which may require the ability to perform time-related calculations.

  It is useful to practise these core skills, as the Maths questions are good question types on which to score highly, since they do not contain any surprise vocabulary. There are many resources available to work through, whether your child is weak or fairly strong in Arithmetic, including games, interactive software and books. You can also do oral maths quizzes with your child whenever you have a few spare minutes.

  It is advisable to work through additional arithmetic questions, other than those in Verbal Reasoning practice papers:

  - To ensure you find any core arithmetic skills that require attention.

  - To improve mental Maths speed so that these question types can be completed quickly, allowing more time for any trickier questions in the rest of the exam. Your child should be able to complete a basic Maths worksheet of 40 questions (mixed operations or times tables e.g. 9 + 8 = __ OR 3 x 7 = __) in less than one minute.

- Increasing Speed

  Improving your child's ability to complete a full test paper in time can be done in many ways, other than just making them do hundreds of verbal reasoning questions (although they will need to do that too). Their ability to process information quickly can be exercised through many games. The Chuckra cards can be very useful, so play a number of games with the alphaCards and numCards which are timed and encourage your child to think quickly. There are also many other online games or family games that require one to think and process information under time pressure, so have fun.

  It is a good idea to improve your child's strengths rather than *only* focusing on their weaker areas. This way they will be able to work through the questions they find easier even quicker and more accurately, allowing more time to spend on the questions they find trickier in the 11 Plus Exam.

Preparation for the 11 Plus Exam is a group effort in most circumstances (11 plus student, parents, tutors, grandparents, siblings etc.), and so I hope this information will help to make the process a little clearer. If you have any further queries, please do not hesitate to contact us. For more information and useful resources, please visit www.chuckra.co.uk

Good luck!

M. Dellocca

Marcella Dellocca

Answers to Verbal Reasoning Types 1 - 21

TYPE 1:
1) GS 2) PV 3) BZ 4) CZ 5) NL 6) BE 7) VW 8) HV 9) RK 10) IE 11) JJ 12) RN 13) IO 14) UL 15) IH 16) UB 17) BK
18) MG 19) IS 20) OB

TYPE 2:
21) TQKH 22) ADAT 23) CEIAXJJ 24) VICE 25) CCBZWMK 26) POLICY 27) ASGFTBF 28) QUOTES 29) HAPPENS
30) YMSXGU 31) PYJLX 32) OFXPB 33) ACTIVE 34) HALF 35) CLOWN 36) PARTS 37) KZON 38) BUCKET 39) LEND 40) DOT

TYPE 3:
41) 63182 42) 62382 43) STALE 44) 82538 45) 85921 46) STAGE 47) 9824 48) 97115 49) PASSAGE 50) 43275 51) 861
52) CAPE 53) YEARLY 54) VERY 55) 12756 56) AGENTS 57) TOGA 58) 84751 59) MEMBER 60) LARD 61) 14537

TYPE 4:
62) ED 63) VC 64) SY 65) YL 66) NH 67) VU 68) SY 69) TZ 70) UV 71) LD 72) CV 73) SJ 74) QE 75) HW 76) YF
77) PW 78) NA 79) DC 80) GY 81) DX

TYPE 5:
82) SIDED 83) OASES 84) DRAIN 85) WRITE 86) TAILS 87) CARTS 88) ELVES 89) SWELL 90) HINTS 91) LINER 92) SIREN
93) SLAPS 94) ENEMY 95) WASTE 96) SALAD 97) EARLS 98) OATHS 99) PHOTO 100) LEAPS 101) STALK

TYPE 6:
102) SALE 103) SEAT 104) LOUD 105) PACT 106) PROD 107) CORE 108) REAP 109) EELS 110) LEAN 111) TWIG
112) BALE 113) PORE 114) IRIS 115) RILE 116) BUST 117) HISS 118) NOTE 119) CAPE 120) EARLY 121) RINK

TYPE 7:
122) WAR 123) ORE 124) TOO 125) TOO 126) PRO 127) LEA 128) ALL 129) PER 130) END 131) HUM 132) URN 133) SUM
134) NOT 135) ALL 136) TEN 137) LOW 138) UGH 139) HIT 140) EVE 141) STY

TYPE 8:
142) just ours 143) that every 144) your ideals 145) even today 146) were very 147) young lady 148) went into 149) at his
150) his own 151) them all 152) Listen to 153) circumstantial and 154) love staying 155) the article 156) This style 157) were always
158) burst out 159) Neither of 160) Rebecca started 161) her sweet

TYPE 9:
162) W 163) I 164) U 165) Y 166) T 167) S 168) R 169) V 170) G 171) J 172) W 173) S 174) F 175) O 176) N 177) F
178) R 179) D 180) W 181) P

TYPE 10:
182) L 183) F 184) P 185) D 186) R 187) W 188) E 189) G 190) P 191) M 192) M 193) M 194) T 195) G 196) M 197) F
198) F 199) H 200) U 201) B

TYPE 11:
202) your self 203) world wide 204) work able 205) was her 206) visit or 207) us age 208) step son 209) store room
210) valid ate 211) upper most 212) under line 213) truth fully 214) trick led 215) stand by 216) track suit 217) to night
218) through out 219) the me 220) as king 221) tea ring

TYPE 12:
222) back front 223) ceiling floor 224) coward hero 225) living extinct 226) cry laugh 227) sweet sour 228) sink float 229) truth lie
230) difficult easy 231) open close 232) awake asleep 233) naked clothed 234) stop start 235) slow fast 236) north south
237) hot cold 238) bald hairy 239) best worst 240) bitter sweet 241) clean dirty

TYPE 13:
242) beaker cup 243) ache pain 244) bough branch 245) broth soup 246) bunk hammock 247) cafeteria restaurant 248) canal river
249) chair stool 250) chum friend 251) forger counterfeiter 252) hairdresser barber 253) giggle laugh 254) obese fat 255) snare trap
256) abandon leave 257) abyss chasm 258) advance progress 259) afraid frightened 260) amend change 261) amiable friendly

TYPE 14:
262) wood plastic 263) sailor postman 264) cage zoo 265) address car 266) music note 267) pauper reign 268) up keeper
269) rhubarb liquid 270) family relate 271) daughter rock 272) side thames 273) neck water 274) forest fire 275) eyes run
276) field player 277) cut wood 278) cream soup 279) game paper 280) food oven 281) weather plane

TYPE 15:
282) sock glove 283) cat sheep 284) four three 285) green red 286) spots stripes 287) rail road 288) foot hand 289) feline canine
290) dollar pound 291) fish bird 292) uncle aunt 293) mouse lion 294) jail hospital 295) horizontal vertical 296) ink lead
297) pig deer 298) television radio 299) morning evening 300) stop rats 301) sun moon

TYPE 16:
302) crowd 303) fire 304) lean 305) rose 306) light 307) calf 308) swallow 309) duck 310) fly 311) count 312) charm 313) peel
314) tip 315) lift 316) roll 317) throw 318) bark 319) free 320) wind 321) part

TYPE 17:
322) E 323) A 324) E 325) E 326) A 327) A 328) C 329) B 330) B 331) A 332) A 333) D 334) C 335) C 336) E 337) A
338) E 339) B 340) B 341) C

TYPE 18:
342) 15 343) 13 344) 240 345) 34 346) 192 347) 26 348) 38 349) 26 350) 1 351) 11 352) 10 353) 32 354) 57 355) 21
356) 16 357) 11 358) 69 359) 7 360) 7 361) 40

TYPE 19:
362) 14 363) 40 364) 101 365) 42 366) 74 367) 39 368) 60 369) 92 370) 67 371) 44 372) 35 373) 38 374) 23 375) 78
376) 22 377) 36 378) 40 379) 12 380) 80 381) 70

TYPE 20:
382) 12 383) 10 384) 8 385) 15 386) 2 387) 8 388) 7 389) 2 390) 4 391) 43 392) 10 393) 35 394) 5 395) 49 396) 9
397) 3 398) 13 399) 8 400) 7 401) 40

TYPE 21:
402) Jason 403) 2 404) green 405) 5 406) 21 407) 6 408) C 409) 19:15 410) Jasper 411) 07:45 412) A 413) 07:40 414) 11
415) 20:57 416) WEST 417) 4th April 418) Kurt 419) 14th July 420) purple 421) B

Answers to Verbal Reasoning All Types Assessment Test 1

TYPE 1:	**1)** LU **2)** IZ **3)** IP **4)** WE
TYPE 2:	**5)** RCKP **6)** STUDY **7)** PILE **8)** HLOV
TYPE 3:	**9)** GANG **10)** SANG **11)** NASTY **12)** 6316 **13)** 8384 **14)** 47517448
TYPE 4:	**15)** WI **16)** EN **17)** QU **18)** JG
TYPE 5:	**19)** TIMED **20)** KILL **21)** PILE **22)** FOUND
TYPE 6:	**23)** NEAR **24)** LESS **25)** NEAR **26)** LISP
TYPE 7:	**27)** RIG **28)** LEA **29)** TOW **30)** ANT
TYPE 8:	**31)** he must **32)** charitably received **33)** These are **34)** dull and
TYPE 9:	**35)** H **36)** J **37)** C **38)** D
TYPE 10:	**39)** R **40)** F **41)** N **42)** L
TYPE 11:	**43)** success or **44)** wrong doing **45)** upper most **46)** take over
TYPE 12:	**47)** accomplish fail **48)** grand humble **49)** continue end **50)** outside inside
TYPE 13:	**51)** lifeless dead **52)** nucleus centre **53)** huddle group **54)** renew refresh
TYPE 14:	**55)** juice pear **56)** tulip grape **57)** knot tighten **58)** frown face
TYPE 15:	**59)** rife kale **60)** roar hiss
TYPE 16:	**61)** part **62)** lift
TYPE 17:	**63)** B **64)** D **65)** A **66)** B
TYPE 18:	**67)** 29 **68)** 72 **69)** 112 **70)** 14
TYPE 19:	**71)** 50 **72)** 8 **73)** 32 **74)** 39
TYPE 20:	**75)** 22 **76)** 56 **77)** 15 **78)** 62
TYPE 21:	**79)** D **80)** Shaun

Answers to Verbal Reasoning All Types Assessment Test 2

TYPE 1:	**1)** AJ **2)** UN **3)** TF **4)** XQ
TYPE 2:	**5)** NICE **6)** REQIW **7)** QKORTV **8)** FAILING
TYPE 3:	**9)** 27739938 **10)** 832135 **11)** SADNESS **12)** 9155 **13)** RAILS **14)** 8176
TYPE 4:	**15)** ZA **16)** GK **17)** HN **18)** JQ
TYPE 5:	**19)** SOLID **20)** LION **21)** DRUGS **22)** SHUT
TYPE 6:	**23)** ONES **24)** SEAT **25)** YELP **26)** VEAL
TYPE 7:	**27)** ACT **28)** NEW **29)** NOT **30)** TEN
TYPE 8:	**31)** her over **32)** some moments **33)** and overcast **34)** it all
TYPE 9:	**35)** R **36)** P **37)** R **38)** P
TYPE 10:	**39)** B **40)** W **41)** P **42)** F
TYPE 11:	**43)** care less **44)** will power **45)** wind fall **46)** err or
TYPE 12:	**47)** great horrible **48)** read write **49)** moderate intense **50)** start end
TYPE 13:	**51)** remorseful sorry **52)** notion thought **53)** elfin slight **54)** insist demand
TYPE 14:	**55)** albatross explorer **56)** cuckoo seaplane **57)** coffee cashew **58)** mango raspberry
TYPE 15:	**59)** sphere cube **60)** shout punch
TYPE 16:	**61)** pad **62)** top
TYPE 17:	**63)** E **64)** A **65)** B **66)** E
TYPE 18:	**67)** 48 **68)** 30 **69)** 80 **70)** 20
TYPE 19:	**71)** 22 **72)** 14 **73)** 95 **74)** 10
TYPE 20:	**75)** 19 **76)** 39 **77)** 47 **78)** 57
TYPE 21:	**79)** 19:15 **80)** grey

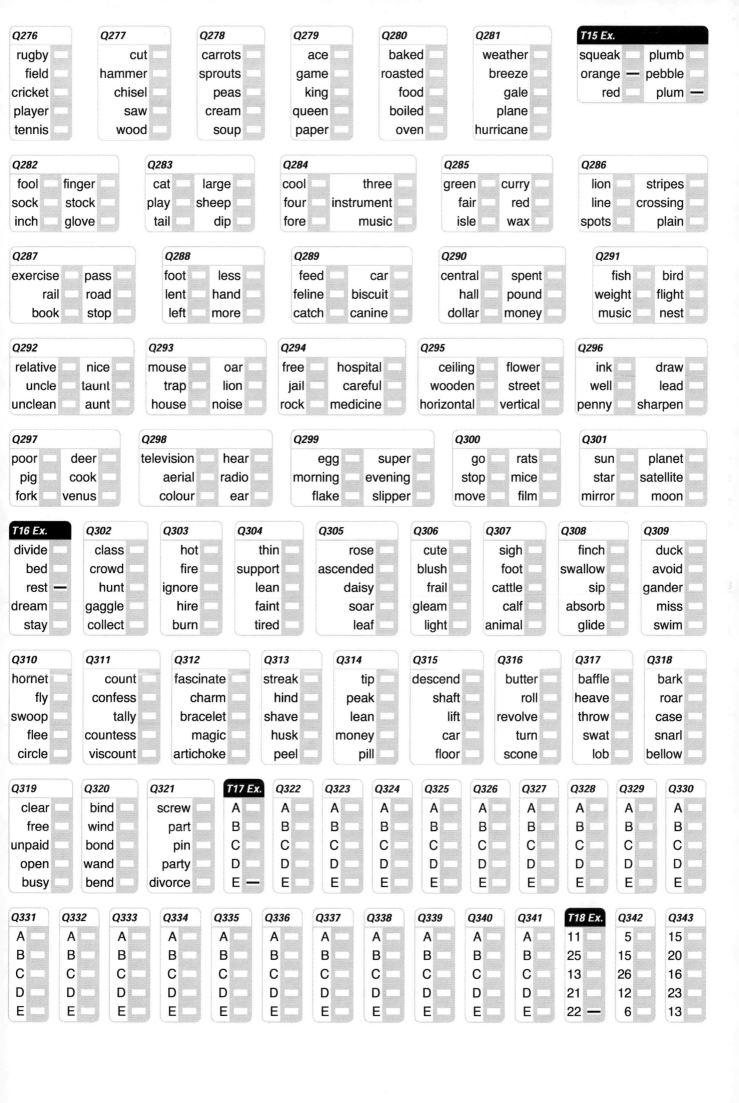

Q276
rugby
field
cricket
player
tennis

Q277
cut
hammer
chisel
saw
wood

Q278
carrots
sprouts
peas
cream
soup

Q279
ace
game
king
queen
paper

Q280
baked
roasted
food
boiled
oven

Q281
weather
breeze
gale
plane
hurricane

T15 Ex.
squeak | plumb
orange — | pebble
red | plum —

Q282
fool | finger
sock | stock
inch | glove

Q283
cat | large
play | sheep
tail | dip

Q284
cool | three
four | instrument
fore | music

Q285
green | curry
fair | red
isle | wax

Q286
lion | stripes
line | crossing
spots | plain

Q287
exercise | pass
rail | road
book | stop

Q288
foot | less
lent | hand
left | more

Q289
feed | car
feline | biscuit
catch | canine

Q290
central | spent
hall | pound
dollar | money

Q291
fish | bird
weight | flight
music | nest

Q292
relative | nice
uncle | taunt
unclean | aunt

Q293
mouse | oar
trap | lion
house | noise

Q294
free | hospital
jail | careful
rock | medicine

Q295
ceiling | flower
wooden | street
horizontal | vertical

Q296
ink | draw
well | lead
penny | sharpen

Q297
poor | deer
pig | cook
fork | venus

Q298
television | hear
aerial | radio
colour | ear

Q299
egg | super
morning | evening
flake | slipper

Q300
go | rats
stop | mice
move | film

Q301
sun | planet
star | satellite
mirror | moon

T16 Ex.
divide
bed
rest —
dream
stay

Q302
class
crowd
hunt
gaggle
collect

Q303
hot
fire
ignore
hire
burn

Q304
thin
support
lean
faint
tired

Q305
rose
ascended
daisy
soar
leaf

Q306
cute
blush
frail
gleam
light

Q307
sigh
foot
cattle
calf
animal

Q308
finch
swallow
sip
absorb
glide

Q309
duck
avoid
gander
miss
swim

Q310
hornet
fly
swoop
flee
circle

Q311
count
confess
tally
countess
viscount

Q312
fascinate
charm
bracelet
magic
artichoke

Q313
streak
hind
shave
husk
peel

Q314
tip
peak
lean
money
pill

Q315
descend
shaft
lift
car
floor

Q316
butter
roll
revolve
turn
scone

Q317
baffle
heave
throw
swat
lob

Q318
bark
roar
case
snarl
bellow

Q319
clear
free
unpaid
open
busy

Q320
bind
wind
bond
wand
bend

Q321
screw
part
pin
party
divorce

T17 Ex.
A
B
C
D
E —

Q322
A
B
C
D
E

Q323
A
B
C
D
E

Q324
A
B
C
D
E

Q325
A
B
C
D
E

Q326
A
B
C
D
E

Q327
A
B
C
D
E

Q328
A
B
C
D
E

Q329
A
B
C
D
E

Q330
A
B
C
D
E

Q331
A
B
C
D
E

Q332
A
B
C
D
E

Q333
A
B
C
D
E

Q334
A
B
C
D
E

Q335
A
B
C
D
E

Q336
A
B
C
D
E

Q337
A
B
C
D
E

Q338
A
B
C
D
E

Q339
A
B
C
D
E

Q340
A
B
C
D
E

Q341
A
B
C
D
E

T18 Ex.
11
25
13
21
22 —

Q342
5
15
26
12
6

Q343
15
20
16
23
13

Q344	Q345	Q346	Q347	Q348	Q349	Q350	Q351	Q352	Q353	Q354	Q355	Q356	Q357
240	31	204	13	35	30	6	11	11	18	50	15	16	10
96	33	60	28	38	34	1	7	7	64	57	18	2	7
256	34	193	35	31	26	14	8	17	32	45	21	20	11
248	29	192	30	33	24	3	23	12	22	51	20	13	25
58	40	18	26	32	32	4	0	10	11	58	22	0	17

Q358	Q359	Q360	Q361	T19 Ex.	Q362	Q363	Q364	Q365	Q366	Q367	Q368	Q369	Q370
54	9	13	41	3	11	54	105	42	85	36	60	91	69
65	7	0	40	18 —	1	40	115	57	65	39	73	100	74
69	8	7	43	19	10	52	101	48	64	41	50	85	55
87	4	1	37	22	14	56	104	50	74	26	64	95	78
68	24	12	48	26	13	50	113	41	75	25	56	92	67

Q371	Q372	Q373	Q374	Q375	Q376	Q377	Q378	Q379	Q380	Q381	T20 Ex.	Q382	Q383
51	51	39	16	78	25	35	41	5	80	62	16	5	15
49	40	25	29	62	8	26	40	4	75	66	18 —	15	10
48	25	38	30	72	27	21	36	12	76	70	19	26	16
35	35	33	23	70	21	36	52	16	71	59	27	12	23
44	26	37	22	89	22	34	35	29	86	79	7	62	13

Q384	Q385	Q386	Q387	Q388	Q389	Q390	Q391	Q392	Q393	Q394	Q395	Q396	Q397
24	21	4	13	5	30	6	21	11	18	4	31	16	10
96	33	6	8	7	34	1	41	7	64	7	48	9	5
56	15	3	9	11	6	4	7	17	35	6	36	27	11
8	29	2	3	3	4	21	43	12	22	5	49	13	3
58	14	8	6	12	2	7	33	10	11	8	28	30	7

Q398	Q399	Q400	Q401	T21 Ex.	Q402	Q403	Q404	Q405	Q406	Q407	Q408
14	9	13	41	No	Mary	1	red	5	4	0	A
13	7	0	40	example	Jason	2	blue	3	8	2	B
29	8	7	43	for	Simon	3	green	17	21	4	C
17	4	8	37	this	Charlie	4	orange	8	42	6	D
28	24	12	48	type	Paul	5	yellow	14	24	8	E

Q409	Q410	Q411	Q412	Q413	Q414	Q415	Q416	Q417
23:30	Scott	06:30	A	06:35	9	20:47	NORTH	7th April
08:15	Jasper	06:45	B	07:40	10	20:23	EAST	7th March
10:15	Mario	07:00	C	07:55	11	20:57	SOUTH	21st April
20:30	Pedro	07:45	D	06:20	12	20:13	WEST	5th April
19:15	Zaeem	08:00	E	07:10	13	20:10	SOUTH EAST	4th April

Q418	Q419	Q420	Q421
Andrew	18th July	red	A
Kurt	14th July	blue	B
Amy	8th July	green	C
Sue	16th July	purple	D
Rich	19th August	yellow	E

Multiple Choice Answer Sheet for Verbal Reasoning All Types Assessment Test 1

T1 Ex.
OV
OC —
CO
VC
CB

Q1
LU
LV
LW
XW
LX

Q2
IZ
BI
IN
IB
NU

Q3
IR
JS
IP
RA
IJ

Q4
WE
DF
HJ
WF
WH

T2 Ex.
LOUT
LOOP —
LOSE
TREE
LAME

Q5
RHXN
RCLB
RCFV
RCRH
RCKP

Q6
STAGE
STORE
STEAL
STUDY
BORED

Q7
PILE
DARK
PITY
PINT
PIPE

Q8
PXFN
HLVD
VDLT
HLOV
HLFN

T3 Ex.
No
example
for
this
type

Q9
FOOT
FONT
GUYS
GANG
FATS

Q10
SANG
FAST
NOON
SAYS
SAGA

Q11
NASTY
STAYS
SNAGS
FONTS
AGONY

Q12
6359
6380
1632
6316
6320

Q13
8353
8380
8350
8384
5055

Q14
47656977
47305518
47809946
69775305
47517448

T4 Ex.
KF
QW
YH
HR
KG —

Q15
WI
VH
WX
WJ
XJ

Q16
EP
EN
DR
BP
EB

Q17
QR
RN
QJ
QU
QN

Q18
XD
JX
LR
JL
JG

T5 Ex.
FACT —
DOGS
MAKE
FACE
DIGS

Q19
TIGHT
VIRUS
TIMED
TITLE
MAYBE

Q20
KIND
BATH
KIDS
KILL
KICK

Q21
PICK
PINK
PILE
DATA
FLAT

Q22
ESSAY
LOCAL
FOCUS
FOUND
FORCE

T6 Ex.
WRAP
STAR
STIR —
STOP
RATS

Q23
NEWS
AKIN
ALSO
NEAR
NECK

Q24
LESS
EONS
LEAP
LENT
LEFT

Q25
SOLE
NECK
ZONE
NEAR
NEED

Q26
HEAD
LIPS
LIFE
EONS
LISP

T7 Ex.
AND
TOP
TIN
FAR —
EWE

Q27
RID
OAK
RIG
RIP
RIB

Q28
LET
LED
NOD
AIM
LEA

Q29
SIX
TOE
TOW
TOO
TOR

Q30
AND
AGE
ANT
NET
TWO

T8 Ex.
Roger paid
paid over —
over the
the asking
asking price

Q31
Now he
he must
must stay
stay by
by her

Q32
Her first
first essays
essays were
were charitably
charitably received

Q33
These are
are our
our real
real turning
turning points

Q34
His complexion
complexion was
was dull
dull and
and yellowish

T9 Ex.
B —
L
O
C
K

Q35
T
H
I
C
K

Q36
F
J
O
R
D

Q37
C
L
O
S
E

Q38
C
A
R
E
D

T10 Ex.
T
E
Y —
S
J

Q39
H
L
R
J
F

Q40
K
V
F
P
A

Q41
N
U
W
V
X

Q42
W
V
U
X
L

T11 Ex.
fresh   acted
habit —   glass
mixed   at —

Q43
success   wins
step   or
bag   image

Q44
wrong   doing
bath   handed
anyone   church

Q45
upper   became
novel   drive
lying   most

Q46
neck   helped
boy   suit
take   over

T12 Ex.
low —   king
pump   high —
sell   bottom

Q47
eye   fail
accomplish   wars
translate   dragged

Q48
grand   cheaper
football   viable
equipment   humble

Q49
liked   end
continue   picture
endings   gate

Q50
pout   called
interior   team
outside   inside

T13 Ex.
save —   king
jump   keep —
sell   hero

Q51
primes   rabbit
lifeless   dead
smaller   lively

Q52
nucleus   adviser
floor   colour
turns   centre

Q53
huddle		group	
shorts		long	
rural		flee	

Q54
remain		gate	
renew		fence	
banner		refresh	

T14 Ex.
octopus	
lion	—
shark	
elephant	—
eel	

Q55
adult	
juice	
youth	
orphan	
pear	

Q56
artist	
tulip	
grape	
blacksmith	
farmer	

Q57
loosen	
release	
knot	
tighten	
untie	

Q58
sad	
angry	
happy	
frown	
face	

T15 Ex.
squeak		plumb	
orange	—	pebble	
red		plum	—

Q59
rife		big	
shoot		swim	
employ		kale	

Q60
king		hiss	
roar		dangerous	
cub		slithers	

T16 Ex.
divide	
bed	
rest	—
dream	
stay	

Q61
serving	
separate	
part	
helping	
banana	

Q62
take	
squeeze	
elevate	
shop	
lift	

T17 Ex
A	
B	
C	
D	
E	—

Q63
A
B
C
D
E

Q64
A
B
C
D
E

Q65
A
B
C
D
E

Q66
A
B
C
D
E

T18 Ex.
11
25
13
21
22 —

Q67
54
39
29
33
27

Q68
114
79
90
69
72

Q69
110
113
130
112
141

Q70
24
14
23
10
44

T19 Ex.
3
18 —
19
22
26

Q71
68
53
49
77
50

Q72
4
56
12
27
8

Q73
45
40
29
32
75

Q74
44
39
38
57
84

T20 Ex.
16
18 —
19
27
7

Q75
23
43
19
35
22

Q76
59
72
96
53
56

Q77
15
18
39
12
28

Q78
60
92
66
73
62

T21 Ex.
No
example
for
this
type

Q79
A
B
C
D
E

Q80
Shaun
Carryn
Hadi
Leo
Jacky

Multiple Choice Answer Sheet for Verbal Reasoning All Types Assessment Test 2

T1 Ex.	Q1	Q2	Q3	Q4	T2 Ex.	Q5	Q6	Q7	Q8
OV	VG	UN	TL	HJ	LOUT	DAMN	REVTR	TQNKHE	QUERIES
OC —	AJ	XD	FI	XD	LOOP —	EVIL	REPNL	QKVSPM	FAILING
CO	AV	UF	LO	DF	LOSE	FEAR	REQIW	QKTQNK	FALLING
VC	RC	UZ	TI	XF	TREE	NINE	VTRPN	QKORTV	FACTORY
CB	AU	LR	TF	XQ	LAME	NICE	REJHF	QKHEBY	TRIVIAL

T3 Ex.	Q9	Q10	Q11	Q12	Q13	Q14	T4 Ex.	Q15	Q16
No	27739938	832135	SANDALS	9155	SMART	8103	KF	XD	HL
example	27801806	838279	LEARNER	5837	RAILS	8125	QW	ZX	GK
for	18061483	467698	SADDLED	9118	RABBI	8680	YH	LR	PT
this	39875878	797234	SELLERS	9172	ALIBI	8186	HR	ZL	GP
type	27483407	832341	SADNESS	9158	ATLAS	8176	KG —	ZA	GH

Q17	Q18	T5 Ex.	Q19	Q20	Q21	Q22	T6 Ex.	Q23	Q24
HN	JK	FACT —	GRADE	GLAD	VOTES	BOOK	WRAP	ONES	SEAT
HF	TQ	DOGS	SOUND	LION	DRUGS	SHOT	STAR	NOSE	TEAS
FN	JN	MAKE	GRAPH	LIES	DRESS	SHUT	STIR —	ONYX	EAST
HP	JT	FACE	SOLID	YOUR	EARTH	HILL	STOP	ONCE	EATS
PX	JQ	DIGS	SONGS	LIFE	DRANK	SHED	RATS	ONTO	SELF

Q25	Q26	T7 Ex.	Q27	Q28	Q29	Q30	T8 Ex.	Q31
PALE	ARMS	AND	PEA	NET	KEG	SAG	Roger paid	Sally threw
YELL	HILL	TOP	ACT	AND	SOT	ARE	paid over —	threw her
YELP	VEAL	TIN	GET	NEW	IRE	TEA	over the	her over
PLAY	IRKS	FAR —	LAX	MEN	NOT	TEN	the asking	over a
DEAD	VALE	EWE	BOO	MOB	BAY	IVY	asking price	a hedge

Q32	Q33	Q34	T9 Ex.	Q35	Q36	Q37	Q38	T10 Ex.	Q39	Q40
There were	The day	He seemed	B —	S	P	G	P	T	B	W
were some	day was	seemed to	L	H	L	R	R	E	L	I
some moments	was dark	to survey	O	O	I	A	I	Y —	J	N
moments of	dark and	survey it	C	R	E	I	D	S	E	B
of silence	and overcast	it all	K	T	D	N	E	J	X	P

Q41	Q42	T11 Ex.		Q43		Q44		Q45		Q46	
P	P	fresh	acted	logic	less	places	nights	flat	states	said	or
J	R	habit —	glass	care	finds	will	power	wind	fall	year	help
B	B	mixed	at —	new	rooms	post	highly	tracks	hurry	err	low
N	F										
H	T										

T12 Ex.		Q47		Q48		Q49	
low —	king	solves	draft	reed	write	angle	colt
pump	high —	sight	pink	right	correctly	moderate	mission
sell	bottom	great	horrible	read	rendered	respect	intense

Q50		T13 Ex.		Q51		Q52	
clothing	end	save —	king	honest	sorry	elephant	thought
start	midnight	jump	keep —	demise	legend	notion	binding
relate	broke	sell	hero	remorseful	please	essence	world

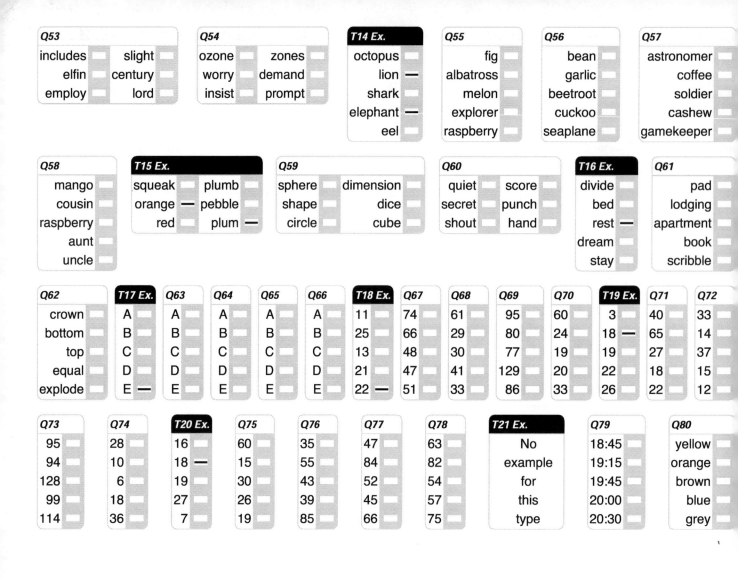

Q53: includes, slight, elfin, century, employ, lord

Q54: ozone, zones, worry, demand, insist, prompt

T14 Ex.: octopus, lion —, shark, elephant —, eel

Q55: fig, albatross, melon, explorer, raspberry

Q56: bean, garlic, beetroot, cuckoo, seaplane

Q57: astronomer, coffee, soldier, cashew, gamekeeper

Q58: mango, cousin, raspberry, aunt, uncle

T15 Ex.: squeak, plumb, orange —, pebble, red, plum —

Q59: sphere, dimension, shape, dice, circle, cube

Q60: quiet, score, secret, punch, shout, hand

T16 Ex.: divide, bed, rest —, dream, stay

Q61: pad, lodging, apartment, book, scribble

Q62: crown, bottom, top, equal, explode

T17 Ex.: A, B, C, D, E —

Q63: A, B, C, D, E

Q64: A, B, C, D, E

Q65: A, B, C, D, E

Q66: A, B, C, D, E

T18 Ex.: 11, 25, 13, 21, 22 —

Q67: 74, 66, 48, 47, 51

Q68: 61, 29, 30, 41, 33

Q69: 95, 80, 77, 129, 86

Q70: 60, 24, 19, 20, 33

T19 Ex.: 3, 18 —, 19, 22, 26

Q71: 40, 65, 27, 18, 22

Q72: 33, 14, 37, 15, 12

Q73: 95, 94, 128, 99, 114

Q74: 28, 10, 6, 18, 36

T20 Ex.: 16, 18 —, 19, 27, 7

Q75: 60, 15, 30, 26, 19

Q76: 35, 55, 43, 39, 85

Q77: 47, 84, 52, 45, 66

Q78: 63, 82, 54, 57, 75

T21 Ex.: No example for this type

Q79: 18:45, 19:15, 19:45, 20:00, 20:30

Q80: yellow, orange, brown, blue, grey

Type 20

For each of the following questions, find the number that best completes the sum.

EXAMPLE

$$12 \times 3 \div 4 = 20 + 7 - [\underline{\quad}]$$

Answer : 18

382. $\quad 11 \times 8 + 40 = 20 \times 7 - [\underline{\quad}]$

383. $\quad 4 \times 6 + 6 = 80 \div 2 - [\underline{\quad}]$

384. $\quad 14 \times 2 - 16 = 2 + 2 + [\underline{\quad}]$

385. $\quad 6 \times 3 \div 9 = 10 + 7 - [\underline{\quad}]$

386. $\quad 44 + 13 + 3 = 20 \times 6 \div [\underline{\quad}]$

387. $\quad 14 \times 3 \div 6 = 10 + 5 - [\underline{\quad}]$

388. $\quad 6 \times 13 - 29 = 7 \times [\underline{\quad}]$

389. $\quad 14 + 16 + 3 = 11 \times 6 \div [\underline{\quad}]$

390. $\quad 64 \div 8 + 3 = 22 \times 2 \div [\underline{\quad}]$

391. $\quad 8 \times 2 - 16 = 41 + 2 - [\underline{\quad}]$

392. $\quad 15 \times 3 \div 9 = 8 + 7 - [\underline{\quad}]$

393. $\quad 43 \times 2 - 16 = 2 \times [\underline{\quad}]$

394. $\quad 6 + 12 - 7 = 20 - 14 + [\underline{\quad}]$

395. $\quad 50 \times 2 - 44 = 2 + 5 + [\underline{\quad}]$

396. $\quad 9 \times 9 \div 3 = 3 \times [\underline{\quad}]$

397. $\quad 14 - 6 - 1 = 2 + 2 + [\underline{\quad}]$

398. $\quad 23 + 13 + 3 = 3 \times [\underline{\quad}]$

399. $\quad 2 \times 100 - 150 = 6 \times 7 + [\underline{\quad}]$

400. $\quad 19 \times 2 - 3 = 60 \div 12 \times [\underline{\quad}]$

401. $\quad 8 \div 2 \times 10 = 48 + 32 - [\underline{\quad}]$

Type 21

For each question, read the information provided and then answer the question that follows.

402.
Five friends are standing in a circle. They are all facing the centre of the circle. Mary is next to Jason and two to the left of Simon. Charlie is to the left of Simon who is on Paul's left.

Who is on Paul's right?

403.
You get into an empty elevator. Two girls get in after you. On the Second floor, one of the girls gets out, but three more people get in. On the third floor some more people get in and four get out. When the doors shut, there are three people including yourself in the elevator.

How many people got in on the third floor?

404.
Jimmy designed his own flag. It had five horizontal stripes, each one a different colour. The red stripe was two below the blue one which was three stripes above the green. The top stripe was orange. Yellow was above red.

What was the colour of the bottom stripe?

405.
Kate is 3 years younger than Martin who will be 17 in 8 years time.

How old was Kate last year?

406.
You are a zookeeper and you are responsible for the elephants. One elephant eats 4 bags of peanuts in 8 days.

How many bags of peanuts must you order to feed 6 elephants for 7 days?

407.
Sammy, a black and white dog, gave birth to a litter of eight pups. Two were black and brown, one was pure black, three were white and black and two were brown and white.

How many puppies had black on their coats?

408.
Zahedah has more pets than Luke who has the same number of pets as Olive. Doron has two less pets than Zahedah, although he has more than Frank.

Which one of the following must be true?
A) Doron has 2 pets.
B) Olive has the same number of pets as Frank.
C) Zahedah has the most pets.
D) Frank has the fewest pets.
E) Luke has the most pets.

409.
Homer wakes up at 08:15 each morning, which is half an hour after Marge. Marge goes to sleep at Midnight. Bart wakes up 2 hours and 15 minutes earlier than Homer and goes to sleep at 23:30. Homer sleeps for double the number of hours as Bart.

What time does Homer go to sleep?

410.
Scott, Jasper, Mario, Pedro and Zaeem go fishing for five days.
Day 1 - Mario and Scott catch 2 fish each.
Day 2 - Jasper catches 4 fish and Pedro catches one.
Day 3 - Scott, Zaeem and Pedro catch one each.
Day 4 - Jasper catches 3 fish and Mario catches two.
Day 5 - Scott catches 2 more than Zaeem who catches only one fish.

Who catches the most number of fish over the five days?

411.
Rachel leaves home at 7:30 and arrives at school at 7:50. Ross only gets to school at 8:00. Joey takes twice as long as Ross to get to school, but arrives at the same time. Rachel and Joey leave home at the same time.

What time does Ross leave home?

412.
Five cars are driving one behind the other along the motorway. Car A is at the front, followed by car B, then C, then D and lastly E. Car C overtakes cars A and B. Car D then overtakes two cars.

Which car ends up in the middle?

413.
Monica caught a bus at 6:30, which arrived at the circus at 7:30. Phoebe arrived at 7:45, which was a quarter of an hour before the show started. Chandler's bus took half as long as Monica's to get to the circus, but only arrived 10 minutes after the show had started.

What time did Chandler's bus journey begin?

414.
Zainub is twice as old as her sister, Priya who will be eight in two years time.

What age was Zainub last year?

415.
My watch is 10 minutes slow. It takes me 12 minutes to shower.

What is the real time at the end of my shower, if I started showering when my watch said 20:35?

416.
You are facing NORTH. If the sun is on your right, which direction will your shadow fall?

417.
Which date is 14 days after the 21st of March?

418.
Kurt is taller than Andrew who is shorter than Amy. Sue is taller than Rich, but not taller than Kurt. Amy and Sue are the same height.

Who is the tallest?

419.
Which date is 18 days before the 1st of August?

420.
Five boys, each wearing a different colour cap, ran a race. The colours of the caps were red, blue, green, purple and yellow. By coincidence, they finished the race in alphabetical order of the colour of their cap, so the boy with the blue cap came first.

Which colour cap came third?

421.
Maddy wears a watch on her left arm and a ring on her right hand. Sean wears his watch on the same side as Zach does. Left handed people generally wear their watch on their right arm. Although Sean is left handed, he does not follow this general rule.

If the information above is correct, then only one of the following statements must be true. Which statement is true?
A) Maddy does not wear a watch.
B) Zach wears his watch on his left hand.
C) Sean and Maddy cannot tell the time.
D) Zach's brother is right handed.
E) Sean is right handed.

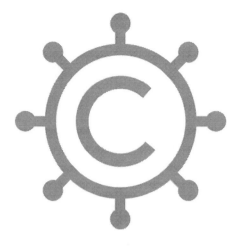

Chuckra Educational

Verbal Reasoning

All Types

Assessment Test 1

This test includes all of the 21 verbal reasoning question types.

80 questions

To be completed in 50 minutes

The Verbal Reasoning practice questions in this book can be completed as either standard version (writing the answers in the space provided on the question pages) or multiple-choice (marking the answers on the multiple-choice answer sheets which can be detached from the centre of the book). Multiple-choice is the more commonly used format.

Type 1

In each of the following questions, find the letters that best complete the series. The alphabet has been provided to assist you.

A B C D E F G H I J K L M N O P Q R S T U V W X Y Z

EXAMPLE

JW KS LO MK NG [___]

Answer : OC

1. VU TS RR PR NS [_____]

2. NL OJ QH TF XD CB [_____]

3. NV KZ ID HH HL [_____]

4. IF OI VM DR MX [_____]

Type 2

In each of the following questions, words have been written in code. The first word and its code have been given to you, but you must find the second word/code. The alphabet has been provided to assist you.

A B C D E F G H I J K L M N O P Q R S T U V W X Y Z

EXAMPLE

If the code for USER is RQDR
What does IMNP mean?

Answer : LOOP

5. If the code for RUDE is TWFG
   What is the code for PAIN ? [_____]

6. If the code for FANCY is UZMXB
   What does HGFWB mean ? [_____]

7. If the code for HOUR is SLFI
   What does KROV mean ? [_____]

8. If the code for PUMP is KFNK
   What is the code for SOLE ? [_____]

Type 3

You have been given four words and three codes. The codes are not necessarily written in the same order as the words and one code is missing. Once you have figured out which word belongs to each code, answer the questions that follow.

OATS FANG TOYS SOFA
1254 7386 3276

9. What does 4254 mean [_____]

10. What does 6254 mean [_____]

11. What does 52678 mean [_____]

RANG MAZE GRIN BANG
8375 5817 6394

12. What is the code for MAIM [_____]

13. What is the code for RARE [_____]

14. What is the code for ENGINEER [_____]

Type 4

In each of the following questions, find the letters that best complete the sentence. The alphabet has been provided to assist you.

A B C D E F G H I J K L M N O P Q R S T U V W X Y Z

EXAMPLE

HU is to FW as ME is to [_____]

Answer : KG

15. XJ is to YK as VH is to [_____]

16. BP is to CL as DR is to [_____]

17. RN is to IM as JF is to [_____]

18. ZZ is to DU as FL is to [_____]

Type 5

In each of the following questions, the word in brackets in the second group must be made from the words outside the brackets in the same way as the word in brackets in the first group is made from the words outside the brackets in the first group. Find the missing word.

EXAMPLE

CLEAN [SAFE] FRESH
ALTAR [_____] CUFFS

Answer : FACT

19. THOSE [HOURS] YOURS
ITEMS [_____] AIMED

20. CURVE [RICE] WEIRD
LISTS [_____] ALIKE

21. BROKE [BAUD] GUARD
PROVE [_____] ALIKE

22. STACK [STUCK] QUICK
FOUND [_____] BUILD

Type 6

In the following questions there are three pairs of words. You must complete the third pair in the same way as the first two pairs.

EXAMPLE

(MINUTE, MENU) (CENTRE, CENT)
(SPIRIT, _____)

Answer : STIR

23. (TESTED, SEED) (VERSUS, RUES)
(MANNER, _____)

24. (ABUSED, BEDS) (LEVELS, ELSE)
(CLOSES, _____)

25. (DEFEAT, DEFT) (CABLES, CABS)
(NEARER, _____)

26. (OLDEST, SLOE) (DETECT, CEDE)
(SIMPLE, _____)

Type 7

In each of the following questions, you are given a sentence. One of the words is missing three consecutive letters, which on their own make a real word. You need to find the missing letters which will complete the word in capitals in the best way to ensure the sentence makes sense.

EXAMPLE

She said EWELL before she boarded the plane.

Answer : FAR

27. But it's all HT

28. Nothing can be CRER than that

29. The band marched through the N

30. He ME to go the other way

Type 8

In each of the following questions, you are given a sentence in which a four letter word is hidden at the end of one word and the beginning of the next word. Find the pair of words that contain a real four letter word.

EXAMPLE

Roger paid over the asking price.

Answer : paid over (dove)

31. Now he must stay by her

32. Her first essays were charitably received

33. These are our real turning points

34. His complexion was dull and yellowish

Type 9

In each of the following questions, you are given two words. Choose one letter that can be moved from the word on the left to the word on the right, making two new words. You cannot rearrange any letters, but the letter that you move can fit anywhere in the second word.

EXAMPLE

BLOCK   RAIN

Answer : B (LOCK   BRAIN)

35. THICK   LATE   _____ _____

36. FJORD   APES   _____ _____

37. CLOSE   HART   _____ _____

38. CARED   RATE   _____ _____

Type 10

In each of the following questions, find the one letter that will complete the word in front of the brackets and begin the word after the brackets. The same letter must fit into both sets of brackets.

EXAMPLE

STOR (__) AMS   CARR (__) ARD

Answer : Y

39. CHA (__) ARE   FA (__) ATES

40. DEA (__) ORMS   TUR (__) LY

41. FLA (__) EAT   BI (__) ICE

42. PA (__) IGHT   REA (__) OAD

Type 11

In each of the following questions, find the two words, one from each group, that together make a new, real word. The word from the group on the left always comes first.

EXAMPLE

(fresh habit mixed)   (acted glass at)

Answer : habitat

43. (success step bag)   (wins or image)

44. (wrong bath anyone)   (doing handed church)

45. (upper novel lying)   (became drive most)

46. (neck boy take)   (helped suit over)

Type 12

For each of the following questions, find two words, one from each group that are most opposite in meaning.

EXAMPLE

(low pump sell) (king high bottom)

Answer : low high

47. (eye accomplish translate) (fail wars dragged)

48. (grand football equipment) (cheaper viable humble)

49. (liked continue endings) (end picture gate)

50. (pout interior outside) (called team inside)

Type 13

For each of the following questions, find two words, one from each group, that are most similar in meaning.

EXAMPLE

(save jump sell) (king keep hero)

Answer : save keep

51. (primes lifeless smaller) (rabbit dead lively)

52. (nucleus floor turns) (adviser colour centre)

53. (huddle shorts rural) (group long flee)

54. (remain renew banner) (gate fence refresh)

Type 14

For each of the following questions, find the two words that are different from the other three.

EXAMPLE

octopus lion shark elephant eel

Answer : lion elephant

55. adult juice youth orphan pear

56. artist tulip grape blacksmith farmer

57. loosen release knot tighten untie

58. sad angry happy frown face

Type 15

In each of the following questions you must choose two words, one from each group in brackets, that best complete the sentence.

EXAMPLE

Pip is to (squeak, orange, red)
as stone is to (plumb, pebble, plum).

Answer : orange plum

59. Fire is to (rife, shoot, employ)
as lake is to (big, swim, kale).

60. Lion is to (king, roar, cub)
as snake is to (hiss, dangerous, slithers).

Type 16

In the questions below, there are two pairs of words. Choose the word from the five possible answers which goes equally well with both the pairs.

EXAMPLE

(relax, sleep) (remainder, others)

Answer : rest

61. (chunk, portion)   (split, divide)

serving separate part helping banana

62. (steal, pinch)   (raise, boost)

take squeeze elevate shop lift

Type 17

For each of the following questions, numbers have been allocated to letters. Work out the answer to the sum and mark the appropriate letter on the answer sheet or in the space provided.

EXAMPLE

A = 3, B = 6, C = 23, D = 9, E = 31
B x D - C = [___]

Answer : E

63. A = 3, B = 12, C = 1, D = 9, E = 18
E - D + A = [____]

64. A = 10, B = 12, C = 6, D = 2, E = 4
E + A - B = [____]

65. A = 2, B = 15, C = 1, D = 5, E = 13
B ÷ C - E = [____]

66. A = 25, B = 20, C = 16, D = 21, E = 33
A + C - D = [____]

Type 18

For each of the following questions, find the number that best completes the series.

EXAMPLE

Example 12 12 13 15 18 [___]

Answer : 22

67. 26 27 25 28 24 [___]

68. 27 30 36 45 57 [___]

69. 67 70 76 85 97 [___]

70. 1 2 3 6 7 [___]

Type 19

In each of the following questions, the numbers in the third group must be related to each other in the same way as the numbers in each of the other two groups. Find the missing number.

EXAMPLE

(3 [12] 4) (7 [35] 5) (9 [____] 2)

Answer : 18

71. (26 [76] 12) (19 [94] 28) (19 [____] 6)

72. (4 [5] 1) (22 [23] 1) (12 [____] 6)

73. (15 [20] 5) (28 [46] 5) (18 [____] 2)

74. (21 [30] 4) (14 [37] 18) (29 [____] 5)

Type 20

For each of the following questions, find the number that best completes the sum.

EXAMPLE

$12 \times 3 \div 4 = 20 + 7 - [\_\_\_]$

Answer : 18

75. $4 - 2 + 27 = 17 - 10 + [\_\_\_\_]$

76. $42 + 3 - 44 = 32 + 25 - [\_\_\_\_]$

77. $14 \times 4 + 33 = 31 + 43 + [\_\_\_\_]$

78. $38 + 43 + 3 = 7 + 15 + [\_\_\_\_]$

Type 21

For each question, read the information provided and then answer the question that follows.

79.

Sonya, Nelly and Britney have to be at swimming practice by 6:00 a.m. every Monday and Wednesday.
Sonya is always late for swimming practice.
On Wednesdays, Britney arrives twenty minutes before practice begins.

If these statements are true, which one of the sentences below MUST be true?
A) Nelly is sometimes late for swimming practice.
B) Nelly sometimes arrives after Britney.
C) Sonya always arrives after Nelly.
D) Britney sometimes arrives before Sonya.
E) Britney is never late for swimming practice.

80.

Jacky has red hair and brown eyes. Shaun and Hadi both have blue eyes. Carryn and Shaun have blonde hair. Leo has the same colour eyes as Jacky, but he has black hair which is the same as Hadi's.

From the information above, who definitely has blonde hair and blue eyes?

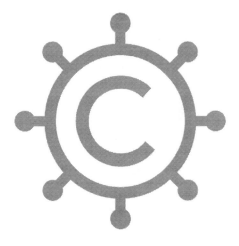

Chuckra Educational

Verbal Reasoning

All Types

Assessment Test 2

This test includes all of the 21 verbal reasoning question types.

80 questions

To be completed in 50 minutes

The Verbal Reasoning practice questions in this book can be completed as either standard version (writing the answers in the space provided on the question pages) or multiple-choice (marking the answers on the multiple-choice answer sheets which can be detached from the centre of the book). Multiple-choice is the more commonly used format.

Type 1

In each of the following questions, find the letters that best complete the series. The alphabet has been provided to assist you.

A B C D E F G H I J K L M N O P Q R S T U V W X Y Z

EXAMPLE
JW KS LO MK NG [___]

Answer : OC

1. EG ZE UD PD KE FG [_____]

2. ZY AY CZ FB JE OI [_____]

3. DF BF ZF XF VF [_____]

4. CH BM AS ZZ YH [_____]

Type 2

In each of the following questions, words have been written in code. The first word and its code have been given to you, but you must find the second word/code. The alphabet has been provided to assist you.

A B C D E F G H I J K L M N O P Q R S T U V W X Y Z

EXAMPLE
If the code for USER is RQDR
What does IMNP mean?

Answer : LOOP

5. If the code for HITS is GKQW
   What does MKZI mean ? [_____]

6. If the code for AWARD is EAEVH
   What is the code for NAMES ? [_____]

7. If the code for FILTER is CLIWBU
   What is the code for THROWS ? [_____]

8. If the code for CONTROL is ZSIZKWC
   What does CEDRBVX mean ? [_____]

Type 3

You have been given four words and three codes. The codes are not necessarily written in the same order as the words and one code is missing. Once you have figured out which word belongs to each code, answer the questions that follow.

DEAR CLAN REDS BADE
5389 7126 8325

9. What is the code for ACCESSED [_____]

10. What is the code for DEALER [_____]

11. What does 9286399 mean [_____]

BARS MALT RIBS CRAB
7346 8159 4176

12. What is the code for TALL [_____]

13. What does 71356 mean [_____]

14. What is the code for MARS [_____]

Type 4

In each of the following questions, find the letters that best complete the sentence. The alphabet has been provided to assist you.

A B C D E F G H I J K L M N O P Q R S T U V W X Y Z

EXAMPLE
HU is to FW as ME is to [_____]

Answer : KG

15. LR is to NO as XD is to [_____]

16. HL is to OS as PT is to [_____]

17. PX is to RX as FN is to [_____]

18. TQ is to PW as NK is to [_____]

Type 5

In each of the following questions, the word in brackets in the second group must be made from the words outside the brackets in the same way as the word in brackets in the first group is made from the words outside the brackets in the first group. Find the missing word.

EXAMPLE

CLEAN [SAFE] FRESH
ALTAR [_____] CUFFS

Answer : FACT

19. HARSH [HEARD] DEATH
BLIND [_____] DOORS

20. COURT [MOST] SMALL
RISEN [_____] OLDER

21. UNION [BEGIN] BEGUN
FIGHT [_____] DRUGS

22. TAPES [SWAP] WORDS
TUTOR [_____] HACKS

Type 6

In the following questions there are three pairs of words. You must complete the third pair in the same way as the first two pairs.

EXAMPLE

(MINUTE, MENU) (CENTRE, CENT)
(SPIRIT, _____)

Answer : STIR

23. (DEMISE, SEEM) (CASUAL, ALAS)
(LESSON, _____)

24. (SECURE, SURE) (LOSING, LINO)
(STREAM, _____)

25. (SPRING, GINS) (IMPORT, TORI)
(PURELY, _____)

26. (DIVINE, VINE) (FORGOT, ROOT)
(REVEAL, _____)

Type 7

In each of the following questions, you are given a sentence. One of the words is missing three consecutive letters, which on their own make a real word. You need to find the missing letters which will complete the word in capitals in the best way to ensure the sentence makes sense.

EXAMPLE

She said EWELL before she boarded the plane.

Answer : FAR

27. The F is, I am not feeling very well

28. He K that Mr Zidane was angry

29. Try AHER Subtraction sum

30. He has WRIT several books on them

Type 8

In each of the following questions, you are given a sentence in which a four letter word is hidden at the end of one word and the beginning of the next word. Find the pair of words that contain a real four letter word.

EXAMPLE

Roger paid over the asking price.

Answer : paid over (dove)

31. Sally threw her over a hedge

32. There were some moments of silence

33. The day was dark and overcast

34. He seemed to survey it all

Type 9

In each of the following questions, you are given two words. Choose one letter that can be moved from the word on the left to the word on the right, making two new words. You cannot rearrange any letters, but the letter that you move can fit anywhere in the second word.

EXAMPLE
BLOCK   RAIN

Answer : B (LOCK   BRAIN)

35.   SHORT   VILE   _____ _____

36.   PLIED   SANK   _____ _____

37.   GRAIN   TIPS   _____ _____

38.   PRIDE   SKIM   _____ _____

Type 10

In each of the following questions, find the one letter that will complete the word in front of the brackets and begin the word after the brackets. The same letter must fit into both sets of brackets.

EXAMPLE
STOR (__) AMS   CARR (__) ARD

Answer : Y

39.   CO (__) LAST   BUL (__) LOWN

40.   CRE (__) ANT   CO (__) AY

41.   PI (__) AYS   PO (__) OOL

42.   O (__) LASH   BEE (__) EW

Type 11

In each of the following questions, find the two words, one from each group, that together make a new, real word. The word from the group on the left always comes first.

EXAMPLE
(fresh habit mixed)   (acted glass at)

Answer : habitat

43.   (logic care new)   (less finds rooms)

44.   (places will post)   (nights power highly)

45.   (flat wind tracks)   (states fall hurry)

46.   (said year err)   (or help low)

Type 12

For each of the following questions, find two words, one from each group that are most opposite in meaning.

EXAMPLE
(low pump sell) (king high bottom)

Answer : low high

47.   (solves sight great) (draft pink horrible)

48.   (reed right read) (write correct rendered)

49.   (angle moderate respect) (colt mission intense)

50.   (clothing start relate) (end midnight broke)

Type 13

For each of the following questions, find two words, one from each group, that are most similar in meaning.

EXAMPLE
(save jump sell) (king keep hero)

Answer : save keep

51.   (honest demise remorseful) (sorry legend please)

52.   (elephant notion essence) (thought binding world)

53.   (includes elfin employ) (slight century lord)

54.   (ozone worry insist) (zones demand prompt)

Type 14

For each of the following questions, find the two words that are different from the other three.

EXAMPLE

octopus lion shark elephant eel

Answer : lion elephant

55. fig albatross melon explorer raspberry

56. bean garlic beetroot cuckoo seaplane

57. astronomer coffee soldier cashew gamekeeper

58. mango cousin raspberry aunt uncle

Type 15

In each of the following questions you must choose two words, one from each group in brackets, that best complete the sentence.

EXAMPLE

Pip is to (squeak, orange, red)
as stone is to (plumb, pebble, plum).

Answer : orange plum

59. Ball is to (sphere, shape, circle)
as die is to (dimension, dice, cube).

60. Whisper is to (quiet, secret, shout)
as touch is to (score, punch, hand).

Type 16

In the questions below, there are two pairs of words. Choose the word from the five possible answers which goes equally well with both the pairs.

EXAMPLE

(relax, sleep) (remainder, others)

Answer : rest

61. (place, house) (notebook, notepaper)

pad lodging apartment book scribble

62. (exceed, outdo) (peak, summit)

crown bottom top equal explode

Type 17

For each of the following questions, numbers have been allocated to letters. Work out the answer to the sum and mark the appropriate letter on the answer sheet or in the space provided.

EXAMPLE

A = 3, B = 6, C = 23, D = 9, E = 31
B x D - C = [___]

Answer : E

63. A = 26, B = 40, C = 17, D = 47, E = 24
D - B + C = [___]

64. A = 9, B = 2, C = 7, D = 5, E = 4
A + C - B - D = [___]

65. A = 10, B = 19, C = 12, D = 9, E = 16
A + C + E - B = [___]

66. A = 33, B = 13, C = 48, D = 35, E = 43
E + C - B - D = [___]

Type 18

For each of the following questions, find the number that best completes the series.

EXAMPLE

Example 12 12 13 15 18 [___]

Answer : 22

67. 58 52 48 46 46 [___]

68. 3 6 7 14 15 [___]

69. 30 40 50 60 70 [___]

70. 1 2 4 8 10 [___]

Type 19

In each of the following questions, the numbers in the third group must be related to each other in the same way as the numbers in each of the other two groups. Find the missing number.

EXAMPLE

(3 [12] 4) (7 [35] 5) (9 [___] 2)

Answer : 18

71. (22 [48] 17) (17 [49] 23) (8 [___] 5)

72. (23 [22] 21) (29 [26] 23) (25 [___] 3)

73. (17 [170] 9) (8 [56] 6) (19 [___] 4)

74. (4 [10] 12) (2 [10] 6) (2 [___] 6)

Type 20

For each of the following questions, find the number that best completes the sum.

EXAMPLE

12 x 3 ÷ 4 = 20 + 7 - [___]

Answer : 18

75. 29 - 16 + 3 = 5 - 8 + [___]

76. 22 + 34 - 8 = 31 - 22 + [___]

77. 6 + 42 - 40 = 31 + 24 - [___]

78. 14 + 12 - 33 = 41 + 9 - [___]

Type 21

For each question, read the information provided and then answer the question that follows.

79.

Ruben leaves home at 18:30 and arrives at the disco at 19:50.
Ross only gets to the disco at 20:00.
George takes twice as long as Ross to get to the disco, but arrives at the same time.
Ruben and George leave home at the same time.

What time does Ross leave home?

80.

Five boys, each wearing a different colour top, ran a race. The colours of the tops were grey, blue, brown, orange and yellow. By coincidence, they finished the race in alphabetical order of the colour of their top, so the boy with the blue top came first.

Which colour top came third?